MILESTONES OF MODERN CHEMISTRY

SELECTED AND INTRODUCED BY

EDUARD FARBER

MILESTONES OF MODERN CHEMISTRY

ORIGINAL REPORTS
OF THE DISCOVERIES

BASIC BOOKS, INC., PUBLISHERS
NEW YORK   LONDON

SECOND PRINTING

© 1966 by Basic Books, Inc.
Library of Congress Catalog Card Number: 66-23492
Manufactured in the United States of America
Designed by Florence D. Silverman

PREFACE

The history of chemistry, like the history of other sciences, has had its dramatic turning points, or, in the popular current expression, its "break-throughs." Yet, curiously, the historic papers that reported these discoveries remain largely buried in the archives, not conveniently accessible to students, nonspecialists, or even specialists, for that matter. Many of them have not even been translated into English. Perhaps efforts to collect anthologies in chemistry have been discouraged by the protean nature of the subject and the fact that the historic papers themselves are often not understandable—indeed, sometimes not even readable—without explanation of the context in which the discoveries were made.

I have endeavored in this book to put together a small collection of milestones in the development of modern chemistry and to indicate the importance of each. Chemistry is in many respects an ancient study whose origins go back about five thousand years. On such deep foundations, chemistry took its modern shape from the work of a few great scientists of the nineteenth and the early part of the twentieth centuries.

The details of atomic structure that account for the chemical characteristics of the elements and the chemical affinities between substances, the nature of the chemical bond, the laws governing transformations of matter and energy—these were the discoveries on which present-day chemical knowledge has been built. Among the men prominent in making these discoveries were Mendeleev, Rayleigh, Ramsay, Richards, Aston, Bohr, Berthelot, Clausius, Gibbs, Lewis, Nernst, Ostwald, and Langmuir.

The nineteen selections presented here, by these and other authors, indicate the development of experimentation and thought in that fertile period. In each chapter, I have briefly related the circumstances in which the papers were written and have tried to supply a continuity. Most of the translations of non-English authors (German and French) are mine; Elisabeth F. Lanzl kindly assisted by translating the papers by Nernst, Ostwald, and Bohr and Coster. The publications are not always reprinted in full; I have selected those parts of the original that are particularly expressive and representative.

Together these selections constitute an inspiring collection of chemical adventures, exciting developments of thoughts, designs of methods, and inventions of apparatus. Emerging from the past, they are fruitful for the future.

EDUARD FARBER

Washington, D.C.
February 1966

CONTENTS

PART I

ELEMENTS AND ATOMS

1

THE PATHMAKERS

Let us attempt to trace the paths leading to the new period of discovery this book records in the words of nineteenth- and twentieth-century scientists.

The paths to modern chemistry begin in antiquity. The ancient artisans carried out many operations we now know to be chemical processes: bricks and pots were baked from various kinds of clay; copper and tin were smelted and combined to form bronze; hides were converted into leather by tanning; plant materials containing sugar and starch were fermented to produce alcoholic beverages. From observation and tradition, ancient workers knew how to distinguish between materials and how to use them for the needs and luxuries of the human body. The search for explanations was left to philosophers concerned with the needs and luxuries of the human mind and heart.

The oldest explanations were founded on cosmic mythology and religious legends. From there the road led to the investment of specific substances with generalized qualities. Thus, in the sixth century B.C., Thales of Miletus, a Greek city in Asia Minor, proclaimed water as the material from which all other substances were made. Around 500 B.C. another philosopher from Miletus, Anaximenes, declared that air, not water, was the primordial material.

In those times it was neither necessary nor possible to elaborate something we would call a valid proof for these ideas. Water and air are essential for our lives; this was the main evidence for the view that water or air was the universal element.

But what about the earth on which we live, the fire we use for keeping warm or for making so many essential materials? Empedocles (about 492–432 B.C.) thought fire and earth deserved equal rank with water and air. Aristotle (384–322 B.C.) accepted and elaborated this system of four elements, which dominated Western science for almost two thousand years.

Prominent among the advantages of Aristotle's system was that it accommodated two pairs of opposite qualities: hot and cold, wet and dry. Was that sufficient to prove that the number of elements should be four? In fact, the Chinese preferred the number five; they included wood and metal, but omitted air. A system of three elements was exalted by Paracelsus in Europe in the sixteenth century. He named as elements sulphur, mercury, and salt. But whatever he understood by these names, the essence of his system was the trilogy or trinity through which this system of the chemical elements could be connected with the deep religious mystery of a tripartite unity.

We should not scoff at these old concepts of elements. Pairs of opposites are still prominent in modern chemistry: for example, the polarity between positive and negative electrical charges. And all our systematic measurements are based on the trilogy of length, weight, and time in the centimeter-gram-second unit defined in the nineteenth century. Moreover, after the discovery of the quantum of action by Max Planck and the absolute velocity of light by Einstein in the present century, physicists felt that a third universal constant should exist. One may suspect that these modern developments are in part connected with still firmly rooted convictions concerning polarity and trinity.

As chemistry grew, the question arose whether the four elements of Empedocles, or the three of Paracelsus, could really be demonstrated by chemical methods. Robert Boyle discussed this question at length in his *Sceptical Chymist* of 1661. His answer was no. Boyle doubted "whether or no there be any determinate number of elements; or, if you please, whether or no all compound bodies, do consist of the same number of elementary ingredients or material principles."

In Boyle's time, the scientists' new-found confidence in the reliability of chemical experiments was the basis for rejecting the certainty of poetic visions like those of Thales and Anaximenes and of the philosophical conclusions put forth by Aristotle and Paracelsus in previous eras. Boyle and his followers found that the presence of these long-accepted "elements" in "all compound bodies" could not be verified by experiment. Therefore the term *element* no longer defined the simplest component in a system of *thoughts*. Instead, an element was now conceived as a *simple substance:* one that operations in the laboratory were unable to decompose.

But were there actually substances that would fit this bold, new operational definition? When the German physician and chemist Georg Ernst Stahl gave a definition of chemistry in 1715, he did not use the word *element* at all. He wrote: "Chemistry is the art of resolving the mixed, or composite, or aggregated bodies into their principles and to combine them again from these principles." Stahl's definition says more than that chemistry consists of analysis and synthesis of substances; it adds that analysis ends at the level where it reaches principles.

What were these "principles"? The word itself implies something that comes first. But first things were not necessarily substances. The term *principle* was often applied to special prominent characters, such as oiliness or acidity. The three elements of Paracelsus—sulphur, mercury, and salt—were interpreted as standing for the "principles" of combustibility, volatility, and fixity. Thus, Stahl's definition was for a while acceptable as a compromise between the old and the new—the former philosophical and the emerging chemical views.

In 1787, Antoine Laurent Lavoisier, often called the father of modern chemistry, removed any remaining indecision in the use of the term *principle* when he accepted the operational definition of an element: "With the name *element* or *principles* of the substances we connect the idea of the end point at which analysis arrives; for us, elements are all those substances which we have not yet been able to decompose by any means . . . and we cannot assume they are composite bodies until the time when experiments and observations provide the proof." In his *New System of Chemistry*, in 1789, Lavoisier listed 34 elements, including some curiosities such as heat, light, and others that were reasonably assumed to exist but had not yet been isolated from their compounds.

So the path begun in antiquity had led from assertion through doubt to new confidence: from a few elements universally present in *all* substances to a great number of elements, only some of which were present in *specific* substances. An operational definition for elements as end products of experimental analyses was necessary, but would even this be sufficient? Since there were now so many elements, could science not characterize each by fundamental properties of its own?

John Dalton had the idea that one such characteristic and fundamental property of an element was atomic weight. He derived this idea from classical Greek philosophy. Leucippus and Democritus had declared that there must be smallest, indivisible particles, called "atoms"—units that could not be further broken down. They believed that atoms were constantly moving in infinite space. From the time of Democritus on, the thought was discussed, explained, and extended by philosophers and experimenters of succeeding European civilizations.

Atoms had this in common with elements: both designated limits. Atoms placed limits on physical division; elements, on chemical analysis. In other respects, however, the difference was great. Chemical analysis furnished tangible results—visible changes in materials, end products. Physical analysis as yet furnished only vague and arbitrary ideas. Could one search for atoms by cutting up materials with a knife? In all the long discussions of atomic concepts up to Dalton's time, nobody seems to have tried to state how a physical division could be carried out or at what precise lower limit it became impossible to effect physical separations. For atoms there was no equivalent to the operational definition that proved so helpful in the theory of the elements. Yet the concept of the atom, though still vague, was deeply appealing. No wonder that it became the playground of imaginative inventions and the battleground of passionate controversies!

Since so little was certain about atoms, Dalton could postulate that the atoms of each element were completely equal among themselves and had a characteristic weight. Naturally, he did not think it would ever be possible to weigh an isolated atom. But that was not necessary for measuring his so-called "atomic weights" in relation to some standard element.

He selected the lightest element, hydrogen, as his standard. He used its "atomic weight" as the unity, or common denominator, by which to express all other atomic weights. The old concept of the atom then helped him in his task, given the additional assumption that nature always prefers simplicity. He assumed that when hydrogen formed a chemical compound with another element, it did so atom for atom. The number of grams of an element that combined with one gram of hydrogen was thus the atomic weight of that element, expressed in grams.

The difficulty here was to ascertain whether the simple assumption of a one-to-one combination was correct. Chemical analysis gave only proportions between the amounts of the combining elements. For example, hydrogen combines with oxygen to form water in the weight proportions of one to eight. If the formula of water were HO, with each of the symbols signifying one atom, then oxygen would indeed have the "atomic weight" 8. But with gases, it is easier to measure the volumes than the weights, and when the volumes are considered the picture shows something new: two volumes of hydrogen combine with one of oxygen and yield two of water vapor.

Early in the nineteenth century, Joseph Louis Gay-Lussac, the great French chemist, discovered that chemical combinations between gaseous elements occur in simple proportions of the volumes. For example, a volume of hydrogen reacts with an equal volume of chlorine to form two volumes of hydrogen chloride. Working from this evidence in 1811, Amedeo Avogadro arrived at the hypothesis that equal volumes of pure gases contain equal numbers of least particles. But these least particles were not always the atoms. Otherwise, the formation of two volumes of hydrogen chloride from one volume of hydrogen would indicate that the hydrogen atoms had been broken in half. Instead of posing such a contradiction to the very concept of an atom, it was more rational for Avogadro to assume that the combining particles of hydrogen and of chlorine consisted of two atoms each. Such particles were molecules, and the reaction was to be represented by the formula:

$$H_2 + Cl_2 = 2\,HCl\,.$$

If hydrogen consists of molecules H_2 and oxygen of O_2, the water reaction becomes

$$2\,H_2 + O_2 = 2\,H_2O$$

and the atomic weight of oxygen is not 8, but 16.

All this was still hypothesis, but it contained hope for the future, or, as Gay-Lussac expressed it in 1809, "that we are perhaps not far removed from the time when we shall be able to submit the bulk of chemical phenomena to calculations."

For a long time, however, Dalton's atomic theory appeared, as Humphry Davy judged, "more ingenious than correct." The real existence of atoms remained far from verifiable by experimental methods. Nevertheless, the concept of atomic weight acquired a reality of its own. If nobody could demonstrate the existence of atoms, at least the relationships between atomic weights and other properties of elements could be discerned. For example, when the specific heat of elements was referred to the atomic weight instead of the gram weight, the calculated "atomic heat" was almost the same for all the elements tested. Thus when some of the elements proved not to fit this new rule, they were considered exceptions as yet unexplained.

Such conclusions could be reached only by dividing one's trust about equally between experiment and hypothesis. The same was true of considerations of crystal forms. Sodium phosphate salts have almost the same crystal form as the corresponding arsenates. They are "isomorphous"; therefore they must have the same number of atoms in the same arrangement in their molecules, and the atomic weights must be chosen accordingly. Although chemical analysis of compounds had yielded only proportions between combining weights, they could be interpreted as atomic weights with the help of other relationships, such as those connected by the law of atomic heat or of isomorphism.

After the time of Lavoisier, many new elements were discovered. Each had its own characteristic atomic weight. While this fact strengthened the concept of the separateness of the elements, the question remained whether this separateness was really absolute; did it preclude any kind of connection between elements? The ancient idea of a primordial matter from which all substances are made was no better founded than the idea of atoms. But, since atomic concept had now found a new shape, should the other idea be completely abandoned?

In 1815, William Prout expressed the thought that the old theory could be revived with the assumption that the primordial matter was hydrogen. The ambitions of other chemists were less extravagant; instead of postulating a common substance in all elements, could they at least find relationships between the atomic weights?

2

DUMAS AND THE
SEARCH FOR ORDER

In the nineteenth century, one group of chemists endeavored to isolate new elements, while another group searched for evidence of unifying links. The aims of the two groups were not contradictory. In experiment, as in theory, chemistry combines analysis with synthesis.

Chemical resemblances between certain elements were already generally recognized; for example, among chlorine, bromine, and iodine and among calcium, strontium, and barium. Most of them came in threes, called "triads"—a strange recurrence of the ancient trilogies in a new shape. An additional link among the members of a triad was that their atomic weights increased in nearly equal steps.

In 1829, Johann Wolfgang Döbereiner established triads like lithium, sodium, potassium and sulphur, selenium, tellurium. He pointed out that the steps by which the atomic weights increased were not quite equal in these series, hoping that further refinements in analytical methods would tend to confirm the anticipated rule.

Jean Baptiste Dumas (1800–1884) thought he had discovered a different kind of rule. When he wrote down the members of one family of elements side by side with those of another family, the difference between the atomic weights of corresponding members turned out to be the same small integer, 5, 4, or 3. Again, this pattern was not completely accurate, but close enough to deserve serious speculation.

Dumas was looking for an orderly scheme in the properties of the elements, for what made them seem to fall into "families." He sought help from recent developments in organic chemistry, especially from the theories of "radicals" and "types." A radical is that part of an organic molecule that remains together during chemical reactions. Thus the methyl radical, or "methylium," CH_3, holds together when methane, $CH_3 \cdot H$, is converted into the chloride CH_3Cl. The integrity of the radical is also preserved in the hydroxide $CH_3 \cdot OH$ (also called "methanol") or the amine $CH_3 \cdot NH_2$.

The "type" theory, on the other hand, emphasized the similarity in all such organic chlorides and derived them from a simple representative, the "type" HCl. Methanol and all other alcohols were of the type *water*, $H \cdot OH$, and the amines belonged to the type *ammonia*, NH_3. These substances thus appear as basic types in which hydrogen is replaced by its equivalent weight of a given radical.

In many respects, Dumas's work marks the end of a period when the main merit of an intuition was its brilliance. Its reconciliation with the facts could be left to the future. Thus he relies on analogies between organic and inorganic chemistry. He assumes that the "simple bodies" or elements are analogous to the organic radicals. Now the differences in the equivalent weights of radicals result from the addition of groups such as CH_2, as demonstrated above. Therefore, Dumas reasons, increases in atomic weights in the elements are also somehow attributable to added components.

And once he lets his imagination run this far, he can also include a hint pointing in the direction of the ancient, universal elements. If the presumably undecomposable "simple substances" or elements of Lavoisier are similar to organic compounds, are they not, then, in fact, probably subject to decomposition?

Dumas elaborates these unconventional ideas in the following selected passages from lectures he delivered in 1857 and 1858. They have been translated from the original French.

◆

The Equivalents of Simple Substances [1]

JEAN BAPTISTE DUMAS

If I have thought it necessary to revise the equivalents of the simple substances, it was . . . because these figures seem to open new and important horizons to natural philosophy by the regular relationships which they reveal.

When we bring together the results obtained for the simple substances and then compare two series or natural families of the radicals in organic chemistry, such as the ammonium- and methylium-derivatives, we find the deepest analogy between them. Thus we have:

				(In the horizontal lines)
Fluor	19	Nitrogen	14	common
Chlorine	35.5	Phosphorus	31	difference
Bromine	80	Arsenic	75	= 5
Iodine	127	Antimony	122	
Magnesium	12	Oxygen	8	
Calcium	20	Sulphur	16	common
Strontium	43.75	Selenium	39.75	difference
Barium	68.5	Tellurium	64.5	= 4
Lead	103.5	Osmium	99.5	

[1] *Annales de Chimie* (3), 55 (1859), 129–210.

				(In the horizontal lines)
Ammonium	18	Methyl	15	
Methylammonium	32	Ethyl	29	common
Ethylammonium	46	Propyl	43	difference
Propylammonium	60	Butyl	59	$= 3$
etc.		etc.		

When the radicals of mineral chemistry, as well as those of organic chemistry, are arranged according to their equivalent weight on a straight line for one and the same family, those for two comparable families are parallel lines.

This analogy raises doubt concerning the nature of the simple substances and would seem to justify so many bold estimates of the probability of decomposing them that I believe it will be useful to say what I think in this respect, while pointing out the network of ideas on which the analogy itself is based.

Today, many chemists follow the course of accepted opinions and do not imagine the fortunate mixture of boldness and prudence with which Lavoisier in his time established the classification of those substances that he had to call simple because the chemical forces were incapable of decomposing them. He put them into five categories. . . .

While establishing the existence of thirty-two substances that are indecomposable by the means then known and, therefore, considering them chemically simple, he (Lavoisier) also introduced the existence of a class of still simpler substances. Of these, five in number, he makes a special class under the title: Simple substances that belong to all three realms (i.e., mineral, vegetable, animal) and can thus be considered as the elements of all substances. They are: light, heat, oxygen, nitrogen, and hydrogen.

I summarize:

The compounds of the three realms are reduced by analysis to a number of radicals that can be classified into natural families. The characters of these families show incontestable analogies; but the radicals of mineral chemistry differ from those of organic chemistry by the fact that, if they are composited, at least they are so stable that all known forces are incapable of bringing about their decomposition.

Nevertheless, this analogy between the radicals of mineral chemistry and those of organic chemistry certainly justifies the question whether the first are composite substances like the second. We must add that the analogy does not give any indication of the means for the decomposition and also that if that decomposition should ever be carried out, it will be by the use of forces or reactions we cannot even imagine now.

As radicals of mineral chemistry, the equivalents of the simple substances all seem to be multiples of a certain unit that would be equal to 0.5 or 0.25 of the equivalent weight of hydrogen.

When the equivalents of radicals of some family, of mineral or of organic chemistry, are arranged in a series, the first term determines the chemical character of all the substances in the series.

Ammonium is represented again in all its essential qualities by the ammonium compounds. Methylium gives its form and behavior to all the radicals of alcohols and ethers. The type of fluorine reappears in chlorine, bromine, and iodine; the type of oxygen in sulphur, selenium, and tellurium; that of nitrogen in phosphorus, arsenic, antimony; that of titanium in tin, of molybdenum in tungsten, etc.

This can be expressed as follows: call a the first member of a progression and d its rate; then in each equivalent $(a + nd)$, a gives the fundamental chemical character and determines the genus, while nd determines only the place in the series and establishes the species.

◆

3

BUNSEN'S
METHODOLOGICAL
LEGACY

Science never was to demonstrate that the elements were made up of chemically separable substances that were the counterparts of radicals in organic chemistry. Nonetheless, Dumas had perceived the probability of an order in the family of elements—an order based on varying combinations of more elementary units of matter than the elements themselves. It would not be long before other scientists picked up the path of Dumas and extended it in a most promising direction.

But before any real headway could be made in interpreting the related properties of old and new elements, chemistry would have to have a more powerful set of tools with which to work. Robert Wilhelm Bunsen, in his experiments with spectroscopy, gave one such tool to the world of chemistry.

In his *Traité élémentaire de chimie,* published in 1789, Lavoisier had listed 34 "simple bodies," but only 23 of these were known as elements. By 1859, the date of the preceding publication by Dumas, 59 chemical elements had been discovered, each one in its own characteristic way. Sometimes it was an unusual color reaction (as with manganese), at other times the peculiar insolubility of a salt (as with the sulphate of barium), that led to the discoveries. Since lithium has a prominent place in the next of our adventures, its discovery deserves special attention.

Lithium's story started in 1817, when Johannes Afzelius Arfvedson analyzed the rare mineral petalite from a Swedish mine. He determined that it contained alumina, silica, and a sulphate. The first part was not at all unusual, but the base of the sulphate was problematic. It was not potassium, because the solution of the sulphate did not give the characteristic precipitations with tartaric acid or platinum chloride. It was not magnesium, because the solution remained clear when potassium carbonate was added. Was it sodium, then? No. On the basis of sodium's atomic weight, the components of the crystallized sulphate would have added up to 5 per cent more than its known weight.

Arfvedson suspected, therefore, that this mysterious base was an unknown element with an atomic weight smaller than that of sodium. Berzelius, in whose laboratory Arfvedson worked, agreed and proposed the name "lithion," after the Greek for stone. He selected this name because he wanted to indicate that the new substance was the first alkali extracted from a mineral. Up to that time, alkalies had been found only in plants—for example, plant ashes—and the so-called "volatile alkali," ammonia, came from animals. Later on alkalies were to be found in many minerals. But the old name, slightly varied to *lithium*, has remained unchanged for this element.

The result of the analysis of the sulphate salt pointed to a new element of low atomic weight. But more corroboration was required. Further purification, plus conversion into the chloride, led other workers to the conclusion that the difference between sodium and lithium should be greater than Arfvedson had discerned it to be. The atomic weight for lithium turned out to be about 7, whereas that of sodium was 23.17, according to Berzelius' calculations in 1814. In 1818, Humphry Davy isolated the element itself by the electrolytic decomposition of the fused lithium carbonate. The method was analogous to the one used by Davy for obtaining the other alkali elements, sodium and potassium, about ten years before.

In 1855, Bunsen improved on Davy's method and obtained lithium in purer form. Even before the new metal had been isolated, the reality of its existence was demonstrated by an optical procedure based on investigations Isaac Newton had begun in 1670. When sunlight is directed through a narrow slit to one side of a glass prism, it emerges from the adjacent side as an array of colors. The prism separates the incoming light into this color spectrum according to the refractive index of the glass, which varies with the "mode of vibration," or the wave lengths, of the many rays that are combined in ordinary sunlight.

On closer scrutiny, many dark lines were found in the spectrum of sunlight. William Hyde Wollaston called attention to these lines in 1802, and eleven years later Joseph von Fraunhofer counted 475 of them. From then on, they became known as the Fraunhofer lines. Fraunhofer deserved this honor, particularly since he also showed that at least some of these lines coincided with those observed in the spectrum of flames colored by the introduction of a salt of sodium, potassium, or lithium. In order to define the places of these lines, he designated them by letters: D for the main yellow line of sodium, A for a red line of potassium. However, potassium showed two lines: one, $K\alpha$, at A, another, $K\beta$, far toward the blue end of the spectrum, between G and H. A characteristic line of lithium was located between B and C.

The presence of this characteristic line in the spectrum made it evident that lithium was an element. On visual, direct observation, strontium appeared to give the same color in a flame, but, as William Henry Fox Talbot stated in 1834, "Optical analysis can distinguish the minutest portions of these two substances from each other with as much certainty, if not more, than any other known method."

And yet, a definite answer remained to be found for the question "whether the bright lines of a glowing gas depend exclusively upon its single chemical components." Robert Bunsen asked his younger friend, Gustav Kirchhoff, for help with the task of finding this answer. For Kirchhoff the request came at just the right time. In October 1859, he had published a "theory for the chemistry of the sun."

Kirchhoff and Bunsen put a few simple parts together into an apparatus with which they analyzed the light emitted by heated samples of salts. Lithium, sodium, or potassium could thus be identified by the lines in their spectra when the corresponding salts were heated in a flame, particularly the colorless flame of the Bunsen burner—the gas-burning device invented by Bunsen himself. Only small quantities of substance were needed for this analysis, and therefore the two workers concluded that their method would make possible the finding of many new elements on earth or in the skies.

In 1861, one year after the publication of the report presented here, the authors discovered two new elements by spectroscopic analysis. The blue line, which they had interpreted as belonging to a new element, prompted them to separate a salt of this element from the water of a spa at Dürkheim. From 44 tons of the water they obtained a few grams of the new substance. Again, a red line, not attributable to any known element, was observed in the flame of a lithium-containing mineral, and the element responsible for the spectrum was also isolated. With their knowledge of the classic languages and literature, they called the first new element "cesium" and the second "rubidium," after the Latin words for blue and red. In the same year, William Crookes discovered a special green line in the spectrum of a mineral and isolated its source, deriving its name "thallium" from the Greek for green shoot. The element spectroscopically discovered in the sun by P. J. C. Janssen in 1868 received the name "helium" from the Greek word for the sun.

Kirchhoff and Bunsen's spectrometer has had many successors. Its beautiful and intricate modern form is not hard to understand for those who have become familiar with the first simple model.

Bunsen was a pioneer in many fields of chemistry. In the following discussion, from a German scientific journal of 1860, the wide range of his thoughts is suggested in what he writes about spectroscopy and its importance for the study of "endemic sicknesses." The report has been translated from the German.

◆

Chemical Analysis by Observation of Spectra [1]

GUSTAV KIRCHHOFF AND ROBERT BUNSEN

It is known that several substances have the property of producing certain bright lines when brought into the flame. A method of qualitative analysis can be based on these lines, whereby the field of chemical reactions is greatly widened and hitherto inaccessible problems are solved. We limit ourselves here to developing the method for alkali and earth-alkali metals and demonstrating its value by some examples.

The lines show up the more distinctly the higher the temperature and the lower the luminescence of the flame itself. The gas burner described by one of us (Bunsen, these Ann. *100*, p. 85) has a flame of very high temperature and little luminescence and is, therefore, particularly suitable for experiments on the bright lines that are characteristic for these substances.

Figure 3–1 shows the apparatus we used for the observation of spectra. *A* is an internally blackened box with a trapezoidal bottom resting on three legs; the two oblique side walls, which form an angle of about 58° with each other, carry the two small telescopes *B* and *C*. The eyepiece of the first is removed and replaced by a plate in which a slit formed by two brass edges is adjusted at the focus of the objective lens. The lamp *D* is arranged before the slit so that the rim of the flame is on the axis of tube *B*. Somewhat below the spot where the axis meets the

---

[1] *Annalen der Physik und der Chemie* (Poggendorff), Vol. 110 (1860), pp. 161–189 (dated Heidelberg, 1860).

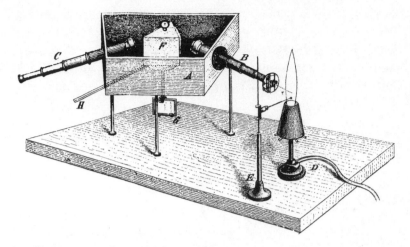

Figure 3–1. The spectrometer of Kirchhoff and Bunsen, 1860.

rim, there is the end of the loop formed in a fine platinum wire, which is held by arm E. The little pearl of the dry chlorine compound to be investigated is melted to this loop. Between the objective lenses of telescopes B and C is the hollow prism F of 60° refractive angle; it is filled with carbon disulphide. The prism rests on a brass plate that can be rotated on a vertical axis. This axis carries mirror G on its lower end and, above it, handle H by which prism and mirror can be rotated. A small telescope is directed toward the mirror so that the observer can see the horizontal scale mounted at a small distance. By rotating the prism, the entire spectrum of the flame can be brought before the hairline of telescope C. . . . Every place in the spectrum corresponds to a reading to be made on the scale. If the spectrum is very weak, the hairline in C is illuminated with the aid of a lens that throws part of the rays of a lamp through a small opening in the side of the ocular tube of C.

We have compared the spectra produced by the above-mentioned chlorine compounds with those obtained when the bromides, iodides, oxides, sulphates, and carbonates of the metals are brought into the flames of sulphur, carbon dioxide, aqueous alcohol, illuminating gas, carbon monoxide, hydrogen, and detonating gas.

In this time-consuming, extensive research, which need not be presented here in detail, it came out that the variety of the compounds in which the metals were used, the differences in the chemical processes of the flames, and the great difference between their temperatures had no influence on the position of the spectral lines corresponding to the individual metals.

Sodium

Of all spectral reactions, that of sodium is the most sensitive. Swan (these Ann. *100*, p. 311) has already drawn attention to the smallness of the sodium chloride quantity that can still produce a distinct sodium line.

The following experiment shows that chemistry has no reaction comparable in sensitivity to this spectrum-analytical determination of sodium. In a corner of our 60 cu.m. room farthest away from the apparatus, we exploded 3 mg. of sodium chlorate with milk sugar while observing the nonluminous flame before the slit. After a few minutes, the flame gradually turned yellow and showed a strong sodium line that disappeared only after 10 minutes. From the weight of the sodium salt and the volume of air in the room, we easily calculate that one part by weight of air could not contain more than 1/20 millionth weight of sodium. The reaction can conveniently be noticed within a period of one second, and in this time only about 50 cc. or 0.0647 g. of air containing less than a twenty-millionth gram per gram pass through the flame, which means that the eye can perceive quite distinctly less than 1/3 millionth mg. of the sodium salt. With this sensitivity of the reaction it becomes understandable that only rarely is a noticeable sodium reaction absent in air at glowing temperature.

This sodium chloride content of the air, which can easily be proven by spectral analysis, deserves attention in another respect.

If, as can now scarcely be doubted, there are catalytic influences that are responsible for the miasmatic spreading of diseases, then an antiseptic substance like sodium chloride could scarcely be without essential influences in the air, even if present only in minimal amounts. By daily and long-continued spectral observations, it will be easy to learn whether changes in the intensity of the spectral lines produced by atmospheric sodium compounds have any connection with the advent of endemic diseases or the direction in which they are spreading.

Lithium

The glowing vapor of lithium compounds produces two sharply defined lines: a yellow, weak Liβ, and a red, strong Liα. This reaction, too, surpasses all others known in analytical chemistry as to definiteness and sensitivity.

With this method, the unexpected fact can be stated beyond any doubt that in nature lithium is one of the most widely distributed substances.

It hardly needs to be remarked that the lines of lithium are shown by a mixture of sodium and lithium salts, side by side with the sodium reaction and nearly undiminished in sharpness and distinctness. When a pearl with a content of 1/1,000 lithium salt is brought into a flame, the red line of lithium appears, although the naked eye notices only the yellow light of the sodium without any reddish coloring. The sodium reaction persists somewhat longer, because the lithium salts are more volatile.

In the technical production of lithium compounds, spectral analysis offers a tool of inestimable value for selecting materials and processes.

Potassium

In the flame, the volatile potassium compounds give a very long continuous spectrum with only two characteristic lines: the first,

Kα is in the farthest red bordering on the infrared, exactly coinciding with the dark line A of the sun spectrum; the other, Kβ far in the violet and also coinciding with a Fraunhofer line. A very weak line, coinciding with the Fraunhofer line B, is visible from a highly intense flame, but not very characteristic.

Strontium

The spectra of all the alkaline earths are much less simple than those of the alkalies. Strontium is especially characterized by the absence of green lines; eight lines are very prominent, six red, one orange, and one blue.

Calcium

The calcium spectrum can be distinguished at a glance from the four discussed above because it has a very characteristic and intense line in green, Caβ. A second, no less characteristic, is the strong orange line Caα, much farther toward the red than the sodium line or the orange line of strontium.

Barium

The barium spectrum is the most complicated of the spectra of alkalies and earth alkalies. Different from the above-described are the easily recognized green lines Baα and Baβ; they are more intense than all the others, the first to appear and the last to fade in a weak reaction. Baγ is less sensitive but still characteristic. The proportionately great extension of the spectrum makes the spectral reactions of barium compounds somewhat less sensitive than the others. In our room, 0.3 g. barium chlorate were burnt with milk sugar; after the air had been thoroughly mixed by means of an open umbrella, the Baα line was distinctly visible for some time. From a calculation like that carried out for sodium, it can be concluded that less than 1/1,000 mg. is indicated by the reaction.

Spectrum analysis should become important for the discovery of hitherto unknown elements. If there should be substances that are so sparingly distributed in nature that our present means of analysis fail for their recognition and separation, then we might hope to recognize and to determine many such substances in quantities not reached by our usual means, by the simple observation of their flame spectra. We have had occasion already to convince ourselves that there are such now unknown elements. Supported by unambiguous results of the spectral-analytical method, we believe we can state right now that there is a fourth metal in the alkali group besides potassium, sodium, and lithium, and it has a simple characteristic spectrum like lithium; a metal that shows only two lines in our apparatus: a faint blue one, almost coinciding with $Sr\delta$, and another blue one a little further to the violet end of the spectrum and as strong and as clearly defined as the lithium line.

Spectrum analysis, which, as we hope we have shown, offers a wonderfully simple means for discovering the smallest traces of certain elements in terrestrial substances, also opens to chemical research a hitherto completely closed region extending far beyond the limits of the earth and even of the solar system. Since in this analytical method it is sufficient to see the glowing gas to be analyzed, it can easily be applied to the atmosphere of the sun and the bright stars. However, a modification is here necessary, because of the light emitted by these stars. One of us in his work "on the relationship between emission and absorption of bodies for heat and light" (Kirchhoff, these Ann. *109*, p. 275) has proved theoretically that the spectrum of a glowing gas is reversed; i.e., the bright lines are converted into dark ones, in case it has behind it a light source of sufficient intensity and sending out a continuous spectrum. It can be concluded that the spectrum of the sun with its dark lines is just a reversal of the spectrum which the atmosphere of the sun would show by itself.

Therefore, the chemical analysis of the sun's atmosphere requires only the search for those substances that produce the bright lines that coincide with the dark lines of the solar spectrum.

For example, the bright red line in the spectrum of a gas flame into which some lithium chloride has been brought changes into a black line when full sunlight is transmitted through the flame.

◆

4

MENDELEEV'S
PREDICTIONS

The discoveries of such men as Bunsen and Kirchhoff gave impetus to the nineteenth-century chemist's quest for order in the growing multitude of elements. Among those who devoted their efforts to this urgent task was Lothar Meyer. At first this German medical doctor who became a professor of chemistry and physics followed the way previously opened by Döbereiner and by Dumas. In 1864, Meyer pointed out that from lithium to sodium to potassium the atomic weights increase uniformly by 16. He compared this with the constant difference between the molecular weights from methyl to ethyl to propyl, which is 14. In an attempt to identify similar regularities and relationships, he arranged 28 of the known elements in a table, so that the differences in atomic weights were either 16 or 45 or 90 (at least approximately) (see Table 4–1).

But Lothar Meyer's main achievement came about through the design of a graph with the atomic weights plotted in numerical sequence on the abscissa (the horizontal co-ordinate) and the

TABLE 4-1

Valence 4	Valence 3	Valence 2	Valence 1	Valence 1	Valence 2
—	—	—	—	Li = 7,01	(Be) = (9,3)
Diff. =				15,98	(14,6)
C = 11,97	N = 14,01	O = 15,96	Fl = 19,1	Na = 22,99	Mg = 23,94
Diff. = 16	16,95	16,02	16,3	16,05	15,96
Si = 28	P = 30,96	S = 31,98	Cl = 35,37	K = 39,04	Ca = 39,90
Diff. = $\frac{1}{2}$.90–45	43,9	46	44,38	46,2	47,3
—	As = 74,9	Se = 78	Br = 79,75	Rb = 85,2	Sr = 87,2
Diff. = $\frac{1}{2}$.90–45	47 '	50	46,78	47,5	49,6
Sn = 117,8	Sb = 122	Te = 128	J = 126,53	Cs = 132,7	Ba = 136,8
Diff. = 88,6	85,5				
Pb = 206,4	Bi = 207,5	—	—	***)	—

atomic volume or some other outstanding physical properties on the ordinate. "The properties of the elements," he decided, "are closely connected with the atomic weight; they are functions, and in particular, periodic functions of the magnitude of the atomic weight." From this, Meyer later developed his theory of a causal relationship. "The numerical figure for the atomic weight," he concluded, "is a variable that determines the substantial nature and the properties [of the elements]. . . ."

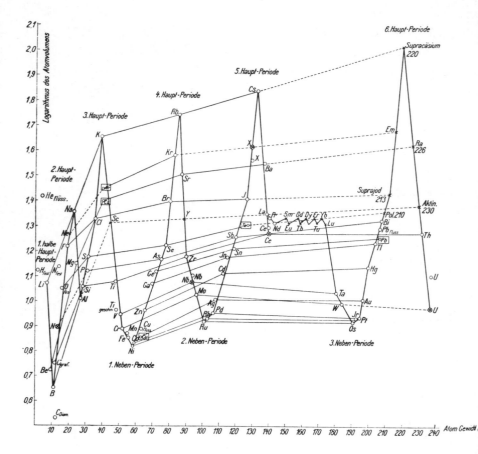

Figure 4–1. Lothar Meyer's graph (by Emil Baur, *Zeitschrift für physikalische Chemie,* Vol. 76 [1911], p. 572). The atomic weights are given on the abscissa, the logarithm of the atomic volumes on the ordinate. The main periods (Haupt-periode) and the minor periods (Neben-periode) are marked. By conjecture, a "superiodine" is entered at atomic weight 213, a "supercesium" at 220.

Meyer's graph is here presented in the modernized form designed by Emil Baur (Figure 4-1). He used the logarithms of the atomic volumes, and he connected the elements of "natural families" by lines across the main graph. These lines of connection between the elements are like the skeleton of the body of new knowledge and theory. The work of Meyer's contemporary, Mendeleev, stimulated the new developments because it gave a glimpse at the shape of this body.

Dmitri Ivanovich Mendeleev (1834–1907) went beyond the search for constant differences in sets of atomic weights. He started from the practical task of teaching chemistry and wanted to provide his students at the University of Petrograd (now Leningrad) with a guide for memorizing the elements. He started to put the elements together in "natural" families and then continued to arrange these families in series.

In arranging his families, Mendeleev's main criterion was the concept of the *valency* of an element, determined by the number of hydrogen atoms that combined with one of the atoms of the element to be classified. In order to establish this number, Mendeleev made a distinction between an element and a "simple body." The "simple body" was akin to a molecule: it could have one atom or several atoms. But by "element" Mendeleev meant the very atom itself. These two different concepts happened to coincide for mercury, cadmium, and some other elements. But for most, such as sulphur, the element was represented merely by S, while the "simple body," which could be composed of two or six atoms, was represented by S_2 or S_6.

Thus, in Mendeleev's scheme hydrogen was introduced as the unit of atomic weight and of valency, and it has remained the common denominator ever since. For example, oxygen ordinarily has two valences, water being OH_2. Any element (R) that has one valence forms a hydrogen compound RH or an oxygen compound R_2O.

Mendeleev's table of the elements starts with the lightest, hydrogen, which appears in a horizontal line all by itself. Below hydrogen are lithium, beryllium, boron, carbon, nitrogen, oxygen, and fluorine, arranged in a horizontal row in the order of their increasing atomic weights. Sodium, the next element according to atomic weight, is not included in this horizontal row; it is placed under lithium because of the chemical resemblance and because R_2O is the formula for its oxide as well as that of lithium.

Continuing in this fashion, Mendeleev finds a periodic recurrence of properties—such as that between sodium and lithium—which leads to the arrangement of the elements in twelve rows and eight vertical family "groups" or columns. There are uncertainties in his table, indicated by the parentheses and question marks. Except for beryllium = 9.4 and aluminum = 27.3, no decimals were given, for they did not seem to be reliably enough established.

The known elements fitted well into this periodic system, which disclosed the regular recurrence of similar chemical properties among the elements as one went up the scale of atomic weights. Therefore the system could be used, Mendeleev rightly believed, to predict atomic weights and other features of less-known elements. Indium, for example, had been discovered in 1863 by Ferdinand Reich and Theodor Richter, who identified it by its characteristic blue spectral line. Yet its atomic weight was in doubt. In the excerpted passages that follow, Mendeleev discusses how a decision can be reached with the help of his periodic system.

In arranging the elements, Mendeleev found it necessary to leave some empty spaces. Since so many new elements had been discovered in the preceding years, it was not hard to predict that others would be found to fill these gaps. Predictions of what these elements would be like chemically could be derived from the system also, since the known elements that were adjacent to the gaps should have congenial neighbors.

This ingenious system was not only numerical but also "natural," in that outstanding properties of undiscovered elements could be calculated in advance. Mendeleev proposed provisional names for the unknown newcomers and, perhaps to indicate how extraordinary it was to do so, he designated them by prefixes taken from the ancient and extinct Sanskrit language. The following selections from Mendeleev's work appeared first in his article written in Russian, then were translated by Felix Wieden in 1872 into German, from which the English version here presented was prepared.

❖

The Periodic Law of the Chemical Elements [1]

DMITRI MENDELEEV

Up to the time of Laurent and Gerhardt the names *molecule, atom,* and *equivalent* were used without distinguishing between them. Similarly, at present the concept of simple substance is often confounded with the concept of an element, and yet the two have to be sharply separated in order to prevent confusion in chemical ideas. A simple body is something material, a metal or metalloid, endowed with physical properties and chemical reactivity. The thing that corresponds to the concept of the simple body is the molecule consisting of one atom (e.g., Hg, Cd, and probably many others) or of several atoms (S_2, S_6, O_2, H_2, Cl_2, etc.). It can exist in isomeric and polymeric modifications and differs from a composite body only by the uniformity of its material parts. Elements, on the other hand, are those material parts of the simple and the composite bodies that cause their physical and chemical behavior. The thing that corresponds to the element is the atom.

The uncertainty in our ideas of valency is in part due to the facts that they have only recently been introduced into science and that they include the hypothesis concerning the combination of the elements through parts of their affinity. In my opinion, this

[1] *Liebigs Annalen,* 8th supplement (1872), pp. 133–139.

uncertainty is furthermore caused by one-sided study of the forms of elementary combinations that disregards the connection with the other properties of the elements. The deficiencies in the theory of chemical composition that are produced by the presently accepted theory of valency will disappear when the atomic weights are used as the bases for studying the main properties of the elements; I shall prove that later on.

Since 1868, when the first part of my book *Outlines of Chemistry* appeared, I have endeavored to solve this task.

I designate as periodic law the mutual relationships of the properties of the elements to their atomic weights applicable to all elements; these relationships, to be developed further on, have the form of a periodic function.

The system of the elements has not only a purely pedagogical significance, as a means to facilitate learning various systematically arranged and mutually connected facts, but also a scientific one in showing new analogies and, thereby, new ways for studying the elements. All the systems known at present can be divided into two sharply separated categories.

To the first category (artificial systems) belong systems based upon a selected few characteristics of the elements; for example, the distribution of the elements according to their affinity, electrochemical and physical properties (division into metals and metalloids); their behavior toward oxygen and hydrogen, their valency, etc. In spite of their obvious deficiency, these systems are, nevertheless, worthy of notice because they have the merit of a certain accuracy and each one of these systems has contributed to the gradual elaboration of chemical concepts.

The systems of the second category (natural systems) arrange the elements into groups of analogues on the basis of many diverse and purely chemical characteristics.

The position of an element R in the system is defined by the row and the group to which R belongs, i.e., by the neighboring elements X and Y in the same row as well as by two elements from the same group with the next smaller (R') and of the next

higher (R″) atomic weight. The properties of R can be derived
from the known properties of X, Y, R′ and R″.

Thus, the properties of all the elements are actually in inti-
mate interdependence. I call the relationship of R to X and Y,
and to R′ and R″, "atomic analogy."

For example, consider an element with the following characteristics: its equivalent is $= 38$ [2] (a figure subject to a certain un-
avoidable error); it forms an oxide that cannot be oxidized further
and is not strongly basic. The question is, what is its atomic
weight or the formula for this oxide? If the formula R_2O were
assumed, then R [atomic weight] $= 38$ and the element would
have to be placed in the first group; [3] there, however, the position
is already occupied by K $= 39$ and, by atomic analogy, it requires
a strong, soluble base. If the oxide were assumed to be RO, the
atomic weight would be 76, and this does not fit into the second
group because Zn $= 65$, Sr $= 87$; all positions for elements of low
atomic weight are taken in the same group. Now if the oxide were
R_2O_3, the atomic weight would be 114 and the element R would
belong in the third group, where indeed there is an open space
between Cd $= 112$ and Sn $= 118$ for an element of the approximate atomic weight 114. In analogy with Al_2O_3 and Tl_2O_3 as
well as with CdO and SnO_2, the oxide of this element must have
weakly basic properties. Thus the element would have to be
placed in the third group. For the formula RO_2, the atomic weight
of R would be $= 152$; such an element cannot be accommodated
in the fourth group because the open place there requires an element of atomic weight 162 and weakly acidic properties (as
transition from PbO_2 to SnO_2). An element of atomic weight 152
could also be placed in the eighth group, but then it would form
the transition between Pd and Pt and would have such striking
properties that they could not have been overlooked; the element
that does not have these properties does not have the atomic
weight 152 nor a position in the eighth group. If the oxide were

[2] It combines in a weight or volume ratio of 38 to 1 with hydrogen.
[3] Under hydrogen, which also forms R_2O with oxygen.

assumed to have the formula R_2O_5, then $R = 190$, which does not fit into the fifth group where $Ta = 182$ and $Bi = 208$, and these are acidic as R_2O_5 oxides.

The formulas RO_3 and R_2O_7 do not correspond to our element either, so that the only possible atomic weight for it is 114, and its oxide is R_2O_3. Such an element is indium.

Use of the Periodic Law for Determining the Properties of as Yet Undiscovered Elements

The periodic law offers the possibility of estimating the unknown properties of elements with known atomic analogues. The tables in which the periodic relationships of the elements are presented show that several expected elements are missing in the periods. Therefore, I shall describe the properties of some prospective elements and thus provide a new and perfectly clear proof that the periodic law is correct, even though the confirmation must be left to the future. The precalculated properties of unknown elements offer a possibility for their detection, since their reactions can be predicted.

In order not to introduce new names for unknown elements, I shall designate them by the next lower analogue in the even- or odd-numbered row of elements of the same group and attach a Sanskrit number (eka, dwi, tri, tschatur, etc.). Thus the elements from the first group are named eka-cesium $Ec = 175$, dwi-cesium $De = 220$, etc. For example, if niobium were not known, it could be called eka-vanadium. In these names, the analogies are clearly indicated; only for the elements of the fourth row they lack this advantage because they have to be derived from the second typical row, which is not completely analogous to the fourth. However, only one unknown element occurs in this row for the third group eka-boron, Eb. Since this follows upon $K = 39$, $Ca = 40$, and stands before $Ti = 48$, $V = 51$, its atomic weight will be about $Eb = 44$; the oxide must be Eb_2O_3 with not very strongly pronounced (basic) properties; it should form the transition from

CaO to TiO_2. Since the volume of $CaCl_2 = 49$ and of $TiCl_4 = 109$, the volume of $EbCl_3$ should be about 78 and its specific gravity about 2.0.

The two elements missing in the fifth row (of the third and fourth group) should have much stronger characteristics. Their place is between $Zn = 65$ and $As = 75$, and they should be analogous to Al and Si; therefore one of them shall be named eka-aluminum and the other eka-silicon. As they belong to an odd-numbered row, they are expected to form volatile metal-organic and chlorine compounds, yet have more acidic properties than their analogues Eb and Ti from the fourth row. The metals should be easy to obtain by reduction with carbon or sodium. Their sulphur compounds will be insoluble in water, and Ea_2S_3 will be precipitated by ammonium sulphide, whereas EsS_2 will be soluble in it. The atomic weight of eka-aluminum will be about $Ea = 68$, that of eka-silicon $Es = 72$. The specific gravities will be approximately $Ea = 6.0$, $Es = 5.5$, or the [atomic] volumes $Ea = 11.5$, $Es = 13$, because $Zn = 9$, $As = 14$, $Se = 18$.

To characterize an element, we need, at present, two data among others that are furnished by observation, experiment, and comparative arrangement; namely, the definite atomic weight and the definite valency. By bringing out the interdependence of these two characteristics, the periodic law furnishes the possibility of determining the one by the other—i.e., the valency by the atomic weight—and, therefore, when the theory of valency defines the chemical combinations, the periodic law defines them, too; but the latter goes a little further in defining also those oxygen combinations that have been left out in the theory of valency.

◆

5

THE PREDICTIONS
COME TRUE—WITH
MODIFICATIONS

At the time when Lothar Meyer and Dmitri Mendeleev developed
their ideas, the problem of a unifying system for the growing
multitude of elements attracted many chemists and physicists.
Most of them placed great importance on the behavior of the
elements in reactions with oxygen and hydrogen. A young French
chemist, Paul Emile Lecoq de Boisbaudran (1838–1912), started
from a different consideration. He was impressed with the development of spectrographic analysis, particularly the work by Kirchhoff and Bunsen. Four new elements had been discovered
through the use of the Kirchhoff-Bunsen method between 1860
and 1863.

Lecoq de Boisbaudran arrived at two interrelated conclusions.
The first concerned spectrum analysis. Since the light emitted by
elements heated to high temperatures is so characteristic, and
since chemical resemblances exist between certain elements,

should we not be able to find resemblances between the spectral lines of those elements that have chemical features in common?

Naturally, the first requirement for work in this direction was to obtain a precise definition of spectral lines. Indeed, such a definition had recently become available. It was based on the work of Newton, who once studied the colors of thin films, like those of oil spread on water, and the phenomena of light diffraction around thin edges. This study had now been developed into a theory of interferences between waves of light. Thomas Young (1773–1829) and Augustin Fresnel (1788–1827) were the authors of this new theory. It was soon confirmed and checked by many ingeniously simple experiments. The wave lengths of light in the visible part of the spectrum were found to range from about 350 to 810 millionths (10^{-6}) of a millimeter. The wave lengths of sodium lines, which Fraunhofer had designated by the letter D, turned out to be 589.5 and 589×10^{-6} mm.

Lecoq de Boisbaudran tried to find simple mathematical relations between wave lengths; for example, in the spectra of calcium and strontium. These calculations were enough to fill his book *Spectres lumineux*, published in 1874. For producing the spectra, he preferred the method of the electrical sparks bridging the gap between two platinum wires to which a trace of the test material was applied.

This search for systematic connections between the elements brought him to a further conclusion: there must be more elements than those already known. Many had been added through recent discoveries, but only a scientific pessimist would have concluded that the limit had been reached. On the contrary, when so many had been found, there must be more. In the same vein, Lecoq thought that a suitable source for discovery would be the type of mineral in which many elements had already been detected. Therefore, he selected a "blende"; that is, a mineral rich in zinc sulphide. Indium had been discovered in one type of blende. Lecoq procured a different type from a deposit in the

Pyrenees and detected, on heating it, some strange spectral lines suggestive of a new element.

He was fortunate in the selection of his method. Working in his own small laboratory, he dissolved the sulphides and then precipitated material from this solution on a piece of zinc metal. He was also very persistent and skillful in acquiring and working up over 400 kilograms of the ore, with the result that he isolated about half a gram of the new metal, confirming his suspicions based on the spectral lines. He named the new element "gallium," from the old Latin name for France.

Some of the analytically important reactions were not as predicted, and a less original investigator would have been led away from the discovery. In certain other properties, however, Lecoq de Boisbaudran's new metal matched almost perfectly one of Mendeleev's predictions. Gallium was, in fact, Mendeleev's "eka-aluminum." Mendeleev had estimated its atomic weight to be 68, and gallium's was 69.72. He had predicted a specific gravity of 5.9; gallium's was 5.94.

Lecoq de Boisbaudran's report is here translated from the French.

◆

About a New Metal, Gallium [1]

P. E. LECOQ DE BOISBAUDRAN

Since the beginning of my chemical pursuits, I have been attentive to the philosophical questions involved in the classification of the elements. Interesting relationships had already been pointed out by several scientists (especially by Dumas) between the atomic weights of certain simple substances and the properties, which invited the chemists to form a natural family of these substances.

[1] *Annales de Chimie* (5), Vol. 10 (1877), pp. 100–141.

I endeavored to find new common features by comparing either the atomic weights of the elements or their qualities, such as, for example, the emission of luminous rays of definite wave lengths at high temperature. Thus I arrived at still unknown relationships, and I drew from them some deductions that seemed quite intriguing to me.

Among the conclusions to be drawn from my attempts at chemical classifications was the probability that unknown elements existed that could fill the vacant places in the natural series.

It is clear that the position of a hypothetical substance in a natural family approximately indicates the properties of this substance.

The uncertainty that exists concerning the exact chemical reactions of a hypothetical substance that is defined only by its position in a natural series renders it rather problematic whether success can be achieved by relying exclusively on such precalculated reactions, because the slightest error in predicting one of these reactions could throw the sought substance out of the place in analysis assigned to it by the theory.

The difficulty seemed very great to me. To overcome it, I devised a particular route of mineral analysis, such that an error concerning the properties of the sought substance or even of known elements would not prevent a final success.

By its extreme sensitivity, spectral analysis is of great help in this kind of work; nevertheless it is not an essential and indispensable part of my method of research. [Spectral analysis] is a marvelous tool, and I have devoted long years to making it more perfect. Before the modifications I developed for the equipment used to produce electrical spectra, it would have been impossible to examine spectroscopically the small quantities of liquid in which I established the existence of gallium for the first time.

My first attempt at a search for new elements started fifteen years ago. At that time I had no laboratory, and my instruments were totally insufficient. That attempt, carried out with considerable quantities of material, had to be abandoned; most of its products were lost. In 1863, my present laboratory was constructed and much better equipped. I renewed my attempts and made a series of studies, but without success. Evidently I had used too little material.

Finally, I decided to operate on a larger scale, as I had done in the beginning of my work, and in February of 1874 I started to treat 52 kg. of blende from Pierrefitte, acquired for this purpose in the summer of 1868.

On August 27, 1875, between three and four at night, I perceived the first indications of the existence of a new element that I named gallium in honor of France (Gallia).

Guided by certain considerations, I admittedly did not wait for the rigorous progress of my methodical analysis. Thus, on August 27, I took some of the white precipitate that started to form in one of my products on contact with zinc foil. This precipitate was dissolved in hydrochloric acid, and the solution was precipitated with excess ammonia, filtered, evaporated, and the ammoniacal salts destroyed by boiling with aqua regia. When the solution thus obtained was submitted to the action of a spark, the spectroscope showed numerous known lines and, besides, the very weak trace of a violet line at 417.0 on the scale of wave lengths.

This line did not exist in any of my pictures of spectra. I did not doubt that I was involved with a new element, and I immediately applied myself to increase my supply of the precious material.

I estimate that the quantity of gallium contained in the small drop examined at the time of my first observation did not exceed $\frac{1}{100}$ mg.

All of the white precipitate that had formed was, therefore, dissolved in hydrochloric acid and treated as described above. The resulting acidic liquid was saturated with hydrogen sulphide, filtered, and again treated with hydrogen sulphide after adding an excess of ammonium acetate. A zinc sulphide separated out which, dissolved in hydrochloric acid, clearly gave the 417.0 line in the spectroscope and, besides, another, weaker violet line near 403.1. Later observations proved that the 403.1 line also belonged to gallium.

After three weeks, I finally accumulated 2 to 3 mg. of gallium chloride, still mixed with zinc chloride.

I then went to Paris where I had the honor, in the last week of September, 1875, to carry out a series of experiments to demonstrate the individuality of gallium in the laboratory of Wurtz before the section of chemistry of the Institute.

Thanks to the kindness of the societies of Vieille-Montagne, Nouvelle-Montagne, and Corphalie, of my learned friend Friedel, and especially of Malgor, the engineer who directs the operation of Pierrefitte for the Société l'Asturienne, I assembled a considerable quantity of minerals, which were treated directly for gallium.

Gallium was reduced to the metallic state for the first time in November, 1875, by electrolysis of an ammoniacal solution of its sulphate.

I have recently put together and treated all the gallium-containing products in my possession; have extracted from it 0.65 g. of pure gallium. Such is the yield from about 435 kg. of raw materials.

I finally united the six samples of pure gallium mentioned before into one quite homogeneous piece. Its specific gravity at 23° (relative to water at 23°) was:

(1) 5.90

  mean: 5.935

(2) 5.97

The prevision of Mendeleev is thus exactly verified.

Among the several hypothetical elements indicated by the ingenious classification of Mendeleev, there is one that seems to refer to gallium in the calculated properties. . . .

I must say that I was unaware of the description given by Mendeleev for his hypothetical element. I should even add that my ignorance has perhaps been favorable to me, in the sense that

I would have experienced delays had I been led to search for gallium in the precipitates formed by ammonia and not in the ammoniacal solutions, which retain it completely, or almost completely, when it is present in small quantity.

The low melting point of gallium also seems difficult to reconcile with what the theory permitted to predict.

Thus, in spite of the incontestable merit of Mendeleev's hypothesis, several reactions and qualities of the new metal differ sufficiently from what the theory indicates to have made it quite problematic whether research guided only by that theory would have been successful when extended to a mineral that is very poor in gallium.

Therefore, it seems probable to me that neither the calculations of Mendeleev nor my own hypotheses would have led to the knowledge of gallium for a long time without the particular experimental method I have followed.

However, the discovery of a new metal now invests the classifications, enabling us to foresee the existence of unknown elements, with an importance they would not have been accorded if no positive fact had come up to support the ideas. I need not emphasize the great interest connected particularly with the confirmation of Mendeleev's views concerning the specific gravity of gallium.

◆

Lars Fredrick Nilson made the second discovery that verified Mendeleev's predictions. The new element was found in a mineral first studied by Johann Gadolin and later named "gadolinite" in his honor. In 1794, Gadolin analyzed this mineral and separated an "earth" from it to which he gave the name "yttria" in reference to Ytterby, the name of the quarry where the mineral occurred. Yttria was an "earth" in the chemical meaning of this word; according to Lavoisier's system it was understood to stand for oxides of metals like those between the alkalies and the heavy metals.

The name "rare earth metals" remains in use for the series of elements typified by yttria.

In 1843 Carl Gustav Mosander demonstrated that yttria contains oxides of several elements. Names for these elements were all derived from Ytterby—yttrium, ytterbium, terbium, erbium—indicating the close similarity of their properties. For the separation of these elements, Jean Charles Galissard de Marignac refined a method Berzelius had introduced. First the earths were treated with nitric acid to obtain the nitrates; then the nitrates were heated to high temperatures. Some decomposed and became insoluble; these insoluble substances could be separated from the remaining soluble nitrates simply by removing the water-soluble compounds. However, the separation was not sharp enough when carried out just once; the conversion into nitrates and their decomposition had to be repeated many times.

One method of testing the degree of separation was to treat the oxide with sulphuric acid and thus produce the sulphate. Assuming that the oxide behaved like calcium oxide, CaO, and took on SO_3 to become the sulphate, it was simple to calculate the molecular weight of the oxide (Nilson often calls it the atomic weight) from the proportion:

$$w : (s-w) = M : 80,$$

where w is the weight of the oxide sample used, s the weight of the sulphate obtained, and M the molecular weight of the oxide ($SO_3 = 80$).

When Nilson carried out such experiments as Marignac had initiated, he noticed that on continuing the operation the apparent molecular weights did not remain constant and differed from the expected values. From these quantitative measurements he concluded that a new element must be present. Additional and decisive tests were made by his friend Tobias Robert Thalén by means of the spectrometer.

Nilson used the traditional right of the discoverer to name the

new element. He called it scandium. Per Teodor Cleve identified
it with the hypothetical eka-boron of Mendeleev.
Nilson's essay is translated from the French.

◆

About Ytterbine, the New Earth of Marignac [2]

LARS FREDRICK NILSON

It is well known how useful for our knowledge of the metals in
gadolinite has been the observation by Berlin, made twenty years
ago, that the nitrates are differentially decomposed when the temperature is raised; it still continues to enrich science in new
results. By applying that observation, Berlin himself succeeded
in obtaining the white earth yttria perfectly free of the rose-colored earth that Mosander discovered in it in 1843; since then,
Bahr and Bunsen, and later Höglund, purified the rose-colored
earth from yttria. This earth, which had been named "erbine,"
was recently shown by Marignac to be a mixture of two different
earths: one of pure rose color and marked absorption bands, the
real erbine; the other white, to which he gave the name "ytterbine." He had too little of the new substance at his disposal to
prepare it in a pure state, but he was led to think that ytterbine
is perfectly white and does not absorb light and that its molecular
weight reaches 131, calculated for the formula YbO.

For lack of material, Marignac had to abandon the further
study of the new earth, and he invited chemists who might have
sizable quantities of erbine to continue this research. I have
devoted myself to this study for some time, the more willingly
since I was at the point of reviewing the molecular weight which
Höglund assigns to this earth (129.7); because this chemist men-
tions, among others he investigated, four that have a higher

[2] *Comptes Rendus,* Vol. 88 (1879), pp. 642–647; Vol. 91 (1880), pp.
118–121.

molecular weight (131.2, 130.4, 129.9, and 129.8). Therefore, I thought that it should be possible to push the decomposition of the nitrate from erbine still further and finally arrive at a higher constant number.

When I began this work, I had in my possession 63 g. of erbine with a molecular weight of 129.25; I had obtained it from gadolinite as well as from euxenite by following exactly the method described by Marignac; however, I stopped heating the molten material as soon as red fumes started to come out, and I thus always obtained crystallized lower nitrates with increased erbine contents. At first, I tried to apply the same procedure for extracting ytterbine from erbine; I found that the molecular weight of the earth that crystallized out as the lower nitrate slowly rose to 130.0, 130.3, 130.4, up to 130.57 (for a very small quantity). This work was so long and exhausting that it seems questionable whether a completely pure ytterbine could ever be reached in this way.

I then used Marignac's process without modification and was successful. After thirteen series of decompositions, heating to complete solidification of the nitrates, there remained a lower nitrate which in the form of the molten nitrate showed only two weak rays of absorption in the green and the red. The solution was precipitated with oxalic acid, evaporated, and gave 3.5 g. of a white earth with a scarcely perceptible rose tint. The determination of the molecular weight gave me the following results:

I. 1.0238 g. of the earth gave 1.6656 g. sulphate (RO $=$ 127.62).
II. 1.0302 g. of the earth gave 1.6758 g. sulphate (RO $=$ 127.66).

I could not explain the results of these two determinations giving the low numbers of 127.66 or 127.62, unless there was a mixture with another earth of a molecular weight below that of ytterbine. Now the problem was to demonstrate the presence of such an oxide and, if possible, to isolate and characterize it. The memoir that follows contains the results of this effort.

Meanwhile, having obtained the molecular weight of 127.6

instead of Marignac's 131, I examined the solutions from which the insoluble nitrates had precipitated.

The mother liquors of fractions 9–17 all contained an earth of molecular weight above 131. They were combined, subjected to the partial decomposition of Marignac's method, and after eight series of operation they gave about 3.5 g. of an earth . . . with a molecular weight of 131.63. By decomposing its nitrate in such manner that the heating was stopped as soon as the initially molten mass became pasty, the last traces of erbine were easily removed. The deposit of basic nitrates contained an earth of molecular weight 131.92 and 132.17 in two different operations:

I. 0.7503 g. of earth gave 1.2053 g. of sulphate (RO = 131.92).
II. 0.7119 g. of earth gave 1.1428 g. of sulphate (RO = 132.17).[3]

The molten nitrate of this earth shows no trace of light absorption; it is, therefore, perfectly pure ytterbine. Marignac's supposition that the new earth would show no absorption is thus completely proved true.

About Scandium, a New Element

The preparation of ytterbine, described in the foregoing note, had furnished me with an earth that was deposited as an insoluble basic nitrate; by extracting the heated mass with boiling water, the molecular weight was found to be 127.6, and not 131, as it should have been according to Marignac. I concluded that the analyzed product should be a mixture with an earth of a lower molecular weight than 131. Thalén, who examined its spectrum, found that its chloride gave some rays not occurring in the known elements. In order to isolate this substance, I carried out several partial decompositions and determinations of the molecular weight of the earth deposited in the insoluble residues containing the new substance.

After the last series of decompositions, the molecular weight had dropped 26 units below 132, the weight of ytterbine; never-

[3] The original here misprints 0.2053 and 0.1428.

theless, the examined product still contained this earth as an impurity. It was impossible for me to carry out any more partial decompositions of nitrates so as to obtain the new substance, perhaps, in perfect purity. Actually, I did not need to have it for demonstrating that a hitherto unknown element was mixed with ytterbine, because the spectrum of this substance, like that of impure ytterbine, sufficiently showed the character of a new element. . . .

For the element thus characterized I propose the name "scandium," which will bring to mind its presence in gadolinite or euxenite, minerals that have so far been found only in the Scandinavian Peninsula.

About its chemical properties, I know at present only this: It forms a white oxide and its solutions show no bands of light absorption. When calcined, it dissolves only slowly in nitric acid, even at boiling, but more readily in hydrochloric acid. It is completely precipitated from the solution of the nitrate by oxalic acid. This salt is very easily and completely decomposed at the temperature at which ytterbium nitrate is partially decomposed. With sulphuric acid it forms a salt that is as stable on heating as the sulphates from gadolinite or cerite and, like these, can be completely decomposed by heating with ammonium carbonate. The atomic weight of scandium = Sc is less than 90, calculated for the formula ScO. . . .

It would certainly be premature to discuss the affinities of the new substance or its place among the other elements; nevertheless, I cannot refrain from making some observations on this subject, guided by the chemical properties that are now known.

Since scandium nitrate decomposes so easily on heating that an almost pure ytterbine was obtained in the decompositions 13–21 of the preceding note, while scandine remained completely in the insoluble residues, it is not possible that the oxide has the formula ScO.

. . . The composition Sc_2O_3 for the earth material is supported by the following facts:

1. Scandine is present in the minerals, together with other rare earths R_2O_3.

2. Solutions of scandium and ytterbium (salts) behave in the same way to oxalic acid.

3. There is much analogy between the behavior of the nitrates of scandium and ytterbium at high temperatures.

4. The double salt of scandium sulphate with potassium sulphate shows that scandium belongs to the same group of metals as those of gadolinite and cerite; all give salts of the same composition.

5. The insolubility of the same salt in potassium sulphate saturated solution indicates that scandium belongs to the cerite group.

6. In the composition of the selenites, the new earth shows much analogy with Y_2O_3, Er_2O_3, Yb_2O_3, on the one hand, giving neutral selenites, and on the other hand Al_2O_3, In_2O_3, Ce_2O_3, La_2O_3, which give very analogous acidic salts, as I have previously shown; I have also obtained a selenite of the same composition from Gl_2O_3.

7. The atomic weight of scandium is 44; this is the value Mendeleev assigned to the predicted eka-boron. . . .

8. The specific heat and the molecular volumes of the earth and of the sulphate place scandium between glucine and yttria.

◆

We saw that when Arfvedson calculated his analysis of a sulphate salt on the assumption that it contained sodium as the basis and found 105 per cent, or a surplus of 5 per cent, he readily suspected that its basis could not be sodium but was actually a lighter element.

Quantitative analysis is more likely to show a loss than a surplus. However, when a skilled analyst like Clemens Winkler (1838–1904), the discoverer of germanium, ends up with 6 to 7 per cent less than expected as the result of miscalculations, he knows that some substance must have escaped and that the usual methods of analysis must be modified if that missing ingredient is to be captured. The methods of qualitative analysis, based on the individual, special qualities of the various substances in a compound, generally utilize differences in solubilities. In Winkler's work, for example, sulphides are produced in slightly or strongly acidic solutions of the unknown material; the products are tested for their ability to form salts with alkalies. Normally such salts are formed with oxides, but here with sulphides, and they are called "sulpho salts" to mark the substitution of sulphur for oxygen.

Dissolved sulpho salts are easily decomposed by mineral acids, but the addition of these acids may also cause a precipitation of sulphur unless the acid is added cautiously and gradually. With a metal like tin, which forms two kinds of sulphides, the "lower" one is converted into the "higher" when it is dissolved by ammonium polysulphide:

$$SnS + (NH_4)_2S_2 = SnS_3(NH_4)_2 \, .$$

Usually the lower sulphide has a deeper color than the higher sulphide. Stannous sulphide, SnS, is brown; stannic sulphide, SnS_2, is yellow. Winkler's new element showed a similar behavior. At first, however, Winkler speculated that the new element was an analogue of antimony, mainly, perhaps, because the mineral argyrodite reminded him by its appearance of some antimony-containing minerals he knew. After some debate, it was decided that germanium corresponded to Mendeleev's eka-silicium, as Lothar Meyer had suggested.

The three elements that corresponded with Mendeleev's predictions were the first to be named for the countries of their discoverers. There was one precedent of an element named after a country, but it was not that of the discoverer. In 1802, Charles Hatchett (1765–1847), of the British Museum in London, proposed the name "columbium" for the element he had found in a mineral that John Winthrop, Jr., the grandson of the first governor of Connecticut, had sent over from America. Berzelius later declared it inappropriate to use place names for elements. With his preference for mythology as a source for names, columbium became niobium.

Winkler's reports are translated from the German. His discovery of germanium served almost as a final proof of Mendeleev's ideas.

◆

Germanium, Ge, a New Nonmetallic Element [4]

CLEMENS WINKLER

In the summer of 1885, a rich silver ore of unusual appearance was found at Himmelsfürst Fundgrube near Freiburg; A. Weisbach recognized it as a new mineral species and called it "argyrodite." Th. Richter subjected the mineral to a preliminary investigation with the blowpipe and found as its main components sulphur and silver, but he also stated the presence of a small quantity of mercury, which is surprising and interesting since this metal has never shown up before in the lodes of Freiburg.

The analysis of the mineral undertaken by me showed that the mercury content is not more than 0.21 per cent; besides, depending on the purity of the investigated material, 73 to 75 per cent silver, 17 to 18 per cent sulphur, very small quantities of iron, and traces of arsenic were found. However, the most careful analysis always concluded with a loss of 6 to 7 per cent, and it did not seem possible to discover the missing part by the usual procedure of qualitative analysis.

After several weeks of painstaking search, I can now state definitely: argyrodite contains a new element, very similar to antimony and yet sharply distinguished from it, to which the name

[4] *Berichte der Deutschen Chemischen Gesellschaft,* Vol. 19 (1886), pp. 210–211.

"germanium" shall be given. Its discovery was connected with much difficulty and painful doubt because the minerals that accompanied argyrodite contained arsenic and antimony; their great resemblance to germanium and the absence of methods for separation were extremely disturbing.

◆

About Germanium [5]

CLEMENS WINKLER

By its appearance alone it was beyond question that argyrodite was a sulpho salt. Therefore, it was probable that the component which so persistently escaped the analysis was similar to arsenic and antimony in other related silver ores. In that case, it was obvious to assume that this component would form a water-soluble sulpho salt when argyrodite was melted together with sulphur and sodium carbonate, and it should then be precipitated from the solution as the sulphide upon addition of acid. Actually, however, operating in this manner always gave only a white precipitate which, after washing on the filter, proved to be pure sulphur, leaving no residue after burning and dissolving in carbon disulphide. In the filtrate, no precipitable substance could be detected either by hydrogen sulphide or by other reagents. I realized only later that germanium really was present in the sodium sulphide solution but precipitated as the sulphide only after adding much acid, because it is considerably soluble in acid-free liquids and thus, once precipitated, could not be washed with water except with great losses or even complete disappearance (by dissolution). The presence of much free sulphur in the precipitate caused additional difficulties. They could be overcome by treating the precipitate, without preliminary washing, by dilute ammonia. Leaving the sulphur behind, germanium sulphide

[5] *Journal für praktische Chemie, 142* (N. F. 34) (1886), pp. 177–229.

is dissolved, and when the solution is then strongly acidified by hydrochloric acid, a white, voluminous precipitate is obtained that cannot be mistaken for sulphur. By adding the hydrochloric acid slowly in drops, first antimony sulphide, then arsenious sulphide are separated; after filtration, a solution is obtained from which snow-white germanium sulphide precipitates upon further, ample addition of hydrochloric acid. Thus, by way of fractional precipitation, I succeeded in removing the interfering companions and in demonstrating the existence of the new element beyond all doubt. . . .

It is now established that germanium combines with sulphur in two proportions, that it forms a brown-red lower sulphide and a higher white sulphide. The sublimate obtained by heating argyrodite in a current of hydrogen is the colored sulphide which dissolves unchanged in potassium hydroxide but goes over into the other sulphide upon treatment with ammonium sulphide. This explains why the addition of acid forms a red precipitate in the first solution, a white one in the other.

The similarity in the behavior of argyrodite and antimony minerals . . . led to the assumption that the new element in argyrodite ought to be close to antimony in chemical character, that presumably its place in the periodic system should be between antimony and bismuth; in short, that it should be Mendeleev's eka-antimony.

It was definitely premature when I expressed such an assumption in my first notice concerning germanium; at least there was no basis for its proof. Nor would I have ventured at first to assume argyrodite to be a sulpho salt with a quadrivalent acid radical, because there were no analogies at all for such an assumption. Thus the present case shows very clearly how treacherous it can be to build upon analogies; the quadrivalency of germanium has by now become an incontrovertible fact, and there can be no longer any doubt that the new element is no other than the eka-silicium prognosticated fifteen years ago by Mendeleev.

Lothar Meyer early declared germanium to be eka-silicium and added that according to his curve of the atomic volumes it should be low-melting and perhaps easy to evaporate. At that time, germanium had not yet been produced in crystallized form; it is so much more remarkable that, as will be shown, Lothar Meyer's prediction has come true to a certain degree.

The specific gravity at 20.4° was found by P. Mann = 5.469, quite in agreement with Mendeleev's calculation, according to which it should be about 5.5.

The tetrachloride is a colorless, thin liquid of specific gravity 1.887 at 18.0° as measured by P. Mann. It does not solidify at −20°. Its boiling point is around 80°. . . . From its composition $GeCl_4$ and its specific gravity, its (molecular) volume is calculated as 113.3; Mendeleev prognosticated the specific gravity of $EsCl_4$ to be about 1.9, the volume 113, the boiling point probably a little below 100°.

◆

These three discoveries, of gallium, scandium, and germanium, demonstrated the value of a system uniting all the elements. The discoveries also showed that the predictions that Mendeleev had derived from his particular system needed correction by experiment, but this is the usual fate of predictions in science. The periodic recurrence, which Lothar Meyer had emphasized and which Mendeleev had further verified in his "natural" system, stirred the imagination of many chemists and led to numerous special ways of presenting the arrangement of the elements.

After the system had been shown to be "natural" and to be consistent with experience, an old question could be asked in a new form: What is the nature of the difference between the elements, and what is added when the atomic weight increases? The long way to the answer will be presented in a later part of our story.

6

ADVENTURES
IN METHODOLOGY

A whole new column of elements was added to the periodic system as the consequence of experiments that started out with the apparently simple goal of obtaining more precise values of gas densities. At first, this seemed to require only improved techniques for a routine task, but in the hands of Lord Rayleigh and Sir William Ramsay it led to the discovery of new gases characterized by exceptional stability. These gases—first argon, then neon, krypton, xenon, helium, and radon—could not be brought to react with any other substance and were, therefore, called the "noble gases." They have now lost this title, because in 1962 it was discovered that xenon could form compounds with fluorine and with oxygen. Other combinations of the heavy "noble gases" with active partners undoubtedly can be formed under certain conditions.

Rayleigh and Ramsay were concerned with an investigation of nitrogen gas taken from the atmosphere and were led to suspect the presence of another hidden gas because of discrepancies that arose when they compared the weight of their sample with the weight of nitrogen obtained from mineral sources. But how separate the suspected hidden gas from the mixture with nitrogen?

Research on air had a long tradition in England. Robert Boyle (1627–1691) published his book on "the spring of the air" (meaning its elasticity) in 1660. Stephen Hales (1677–1761) devised many improvements in the methods of handling separate volumes of gases. Joseph Priestley (1733–1804) used a eudiometer to test the "goodness" of air. And more than a century before the work by Ramsay and Rayleigh, Henry Cavendish (1731–1810) had measured the proportion of "dephlogisticated" to "phlogisticated" air.[1]

Cavendish did not like the then modern terms "oxygen" and "nitrogen."[2] His method consisted in passing electric sparks through the mixture and removing the nitrous gas which formed by "absorbing" (dissolving) it in water, or preferably in "lees," a solution of potash. Then he continued the sparking after adding more oxygen in such proportions that all the nitrogen and all the oxygen combined with each other. But, although he made sure that neither one nor the other remained, he still found a small residue. In his experiments, this residue amounted to only $\frac{1}{120}$ part of the nitrogen; yet even that was worth reporting, and Cavendish concluded: ". . . so that if there is any part of the phlogisticated air of our atmosphere which differs from the rest, and cannot be reduced to nitrous acid, we may safely conclude, that it is not more than $\frac{1}{120}$ part of the whole" (1784).

William Ramsay (1852–1916) remembered reading this passage when Lord Rayleigh (1842–1919) asked his opinion about a

---

[1] In Cavendish's day, scientists interpreted atmospheric gases in the terms of Georg Ernst Stahl. Stahl had given to the old alchemical idea of a "burning principle" the name "phlogiston." When a substance burned, the phlogiston was presumed to leave it, escaping into the air. Cavendish, who isolated hydrogen, believed that he had isolated phlogiston itself as the result of treating metals with acids. In each case, the resultant gas burned readily with a dim blue flame.

[2] Oxygen was isolated in 1774 by Priestley and even earlier by Scheele, without fully understanding what they had; nitrogen, in 1772 by Rutherford.

strange experimental result. Lord Rayleigh had measured the specific gravity of various gases, among them oxygen and nitrogen. In order to make sure that he had pure materials, he prepared them in different ways. Thus, he prepared oxygen from potassium chlorate or permanganate and, in addition, by electrolysis. The specific gravity was always the same. But when he compared the nitrogen prepared from air with the nitrogen obtained from its chemical compounds, he found the latter slightly but distinctly lighter.

Rayleigh supposed that "chemical nitrogen" was contaminated by a gas *lighter* than real nitrogen. Ramsay, however, with Cavendish's experiment in mind, thought that the "atmospheric nitrogen" contained a *heavier* gas of unknown nature. They joined forces to solve the problem.

In their method, they used a "globe," a spherical glass container with a narrow neck connected with a stopcock and a very accurate manometer. The glass was immersed in an ice-water mixture to keep it at 0° C.; then the air in the globe was pumped out, and gas was admitted until it reached the normal pressure of the atmosphere.

The measuring was done against a slightly heavier counterweight, so that weights had to be added to the side of the globe. Therefore, the "empty," i.e., evacuated, globe required the addition to its side of more weight than the "full" globe containing the test gas (see page 59). The weighings were so precise that even the slight shrinkage of the globe because of the vacuum (that is, under the outside pressure of the atmosphere) had to be considered. Since the volume of the container was known from weighing it with water (1836.5 g.), the weight per liter could be calculated; for chemical nitrogen this weight was 1.2505, for atmospheric nitrogen 1.2572.

The difference was firmly established. The experiments had to decide between the opposite conjectures of the two authors. Even that was not enough, however. Still a third possibility had to be considered; namely, was the contaminating gas produced by the operations used in preparing the gases? In such cases, the gas would be an artifact and not a substance that existed in the undisturbed, normal air.

One part of the answer came out of the beautifully designed experiment, in which atmospheric nitrogen was converted into "chemical" nitrogen by way of its chemical compound with magnesium, the magnesium nitride. Another suspicion was removed by avoiding "hot metals"; that is, the purification of the gas was not carried out by the traditional method of passing it over a layer of heated copper (which normally removed any traces of remaining oxygen or other reactive impurities).

One possibility was that the molecules of nitrogen, which consists of two atoms of N as N_2, dissociated under the influence of the electric sparks to form the lighter monatomic gas N. A long period at room temperature would have restored the normal state of N_2. But it was found that the freshly sparked product had the same specific gravity as the aged one, eliminating this possibility as well.

And so the decision was reached to prepare the contaminant gas in sizable and analyzable quantities. It turned out to be a heavy new gas. It was found to be a monatomic gas by the ratio of two measurements of its specific heat: one measurement was taken when the gas was permitted to expand freely as it was heated, preserving constant pressure; the other was taken when the volume was kept constant.

A method that certainly could not be suspected of manufacturing anything that was not there at the start of the experiment was diffusion of air through the fine pores of clay pipes. The smaller molecules of the lighter gas would go through these tiny pores more easily than those of the heavier component, so that this heavier gas was accumulated in the pipes.

William Crookes (1832–1919), the expert on the spectra of gases, was called in. He verified that this was a new gas. When, soon afterward, Ramsay and Travers discovered the gases helium, neon, and krypton in the atmosphere, they were found to be as unreactive as argon. Their place in the periodic system could not, therefore, be in any of the columns arranged by reactivity, least of all in the last column, which contained substances that had up to eight valences—the octad. Crookes devised a scheme of arrangement in a "figure of eight," a winding spiral, which is shown in the accompanying Figure 6–1.

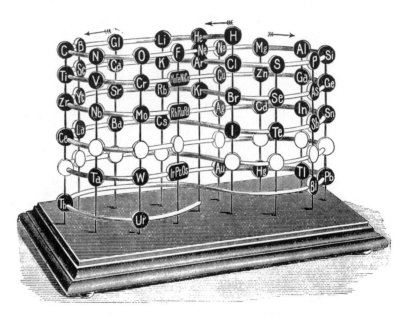

Figure 6–1. The periodic system according to Sir William Crookes (*Proceedings of the Royal Society,* Vol. 63 [1898], p. 409).

◆

Argon, a New Constituent of the Atmosphere[3]

LORD RAYLEIGH AND WILLIAM RAMSAY

Density of Nitrogen from Various Sources

In a former paper [*] it has been shown that nitrogen extracted from chemical compounds is about ½ per cent lighter than "atmospheric nitrogen."

The mean number for the weights of gas contained in the globe used were as follows:

	Grams
	Grams
From nitric oxide	2.3001
From nitrous oxide	2.2990
From ammonium nitrite	2.2987

while for "atmospheric nitrogen" there was found:

	Grams
	Grams
By hot copper, 1892	2.3103
By hot iron, 1893	2.3100
By ferrous hydrate, 1894	2.3102

To the above list may be added nitrogen prepared in yet another manner, whose weight has been determined subsequently to the isolation of the new dense constituent of the atmosphere. In this case, nitrogen was actually extracted from air by means of magnesium. The nitrogen thus separated was then converted into ammonia by action of water upon the magnesium nitride and

---

[3] Abstract of a paper received at the Royal Society on January 31, 1895.

[*] Rayleigh, "On the Densities of the Principal Gases," *Proceedings of the Royal Society*, Vol. 53 (1893), p. 134.

afterwards liberated in the free state by means of calcium hypochlorite. The purification was conducted in the usual way, including passage over red-hot copper and copper oxide. The following was the result:

	Grams
Globe empty, Oct. 30, Nov. 5	2.82313
Globe full, Oct. 31	0.52395
Weight of gas	2.29918

It differs inappreciably from the mean of other results, viz., 2.2990, and is of special interest as relating to gas which at one stage of its history formed part of the atmosphere.

Another determination, with a different apparatus, of the density of "chemical" nitrogen from the same source, magnesium nitride, which had been prepared by passing "atmospheric" nitrogen over ignited magnesium, may here be recorded. The sample differed from that previously mentioned, inasmuch as it had not been subjected to treatment with red-hot copper. After treating the nitride with water, the resulting ammonia was distilled off and collected in hydrochloric acid; the solution was evaporated by degrees, the dry ammonium chloride was dissolved in water, and its concentrated solution added to a freshly prepared solution of sodium hypobromite. The nitrogen was collected in a gas holder over water which had previously been boiled, so as, at all events partially, to expel air. The nitrogen passed into the vacuous globe through a solution of potassium hydroxide and through two drying tubes, one containing soda-lime and the other phosphoric anhydride.

At 18.38° C. and 754.4 mm. pressure, 162.843 cc. of this nitrogen weighed 0.18963 gram. Hence, weight of 1 litre at 0° C. and 760 mm. pressure = 1.2521 gram.

The mean result of the weight of 1 litre of "chemical" nitrogen has been found to equal 1.2505. It is therefore seen that "chemical" nitrogen, derived from "atmospheric" nitrogen, without any exposure to red-hot copper, possesses about the usual density.

Experiments were also made which had for their object to prove that the ammonia produced from the magnesium nitride is identical with ordinary ammonia and contains no other compound of a basic character. For this purpose, the ammonia was converted into ammonium chloride, and the percentage of chlorine determined by titration with a solution of silver nitrate which had been standardized by titrating a specimen of pure sublimed ammonium chloride. The silver solution was of such a strength that 1 cc. precipitated the chlorine from 0.001701 g. of ammonium chloride.

1. Ammonium chloride from orange-coloured sample of magnesium nitride contained 66.35 per cent of chlorine.

2. Ammonium chloride from blackish magnesium nitride contained 66.35 per cent of chlorine.

3. Ammonium chloride from nitride containing a large amount of unattacked magnesium contained 66.30 per cent of chlorine.

Taking for the atomic weights of hydrogen $H = 1.0032$, of nitrogen $N = 14.04$, and of chlorine $Cl = 35.46$, the theoretical amount of chlorine in ammonium chloride is 66.27 per cent.

From these results—that nitrogen prepared from magnesium nitride, obtained by passing "atmospheric" nitrogen over red-hot magnesium, has the density of "chemical" nitrogen, and that ammonium chloride, prepared from magnesium nitride, contains practically the same percentage of chlorine as pure ammonium chloride—it may be concluded that red-hot magnesium withdraws from "atmospheric nitrogen" no substance other than nitrogen capable of forming a basic compound with hydrogen.

Reasons for Suspecting a Hitherto Undiscovered Constituent in Air

When the discrepancy of weights was first encountered, attempts were naturally made to explain it by contamination with known impurities. Of these the most likely appeared to be hydrogen, present in the lighter gas in spite of the passage over redhot cupric oxide. But inasmuch as the intentional introduction of hydrogen into the heavier gas, afterward treated in the same way with cupric oxide, had no effect upon its weight, this explanation had to be abandoned, and finally it became clear that the difference could not be accounted for by the presence of any known impurity. At this stage, it seemed not improbable that the lightness of the gas extracted from chemical compounds was to be explained by partial dissociation of nitrogen molecules N_2 into detached atoms. In order to test this suggestion, both kinds of gas were submitted to the action of the silent electric discharge, with the result that both retained their weights unaltered. This was discouraging, and a further experiment pointed still more markedly in the negative direction. The chemical behaviour of nitrogen is such as to suggest that dissociated atoms would possess a high degree of activity and that even though they might be formed in the first instance, their life would probably be short. On standing, they might be expected to disappear, in partial analogy with the known behaviour of ozone. With this idea in view, a sample of chemically prepared nitrogen was stored for eight months. But at the end of this time the density showed no sign of increase, remaining exactly as at first.*

Regarding it as established that one or other of the gases must be a mixture, containing, as the case might be, an ingredient much heavier or much lighter than ordinary nitrogen, we had to consider the relative probabilities of the various possible interpretations. Except upon the already discredited hypothesis of dissociation, it was difficult to see how the gas of chemical origin could be a mixture. To suppose this would be to admit two kinds of nitric acid, hardly reconcilable with the work of Stas and others upon the atomic weight of that substance. The simplest explanation in many respects was to admit the existence of a second ingredient in air from which oxygen, moisture, and carbonic anhydride had already been removed. The proportional

* *Ibid.*, Vol. 55 (1894), p. 344.

amount required was not great. If the density of the supposed gas were double that of nitrogen, ½ per cent only by volume would be needed; or if the density were but half as much again as that of nitrogen, then 1 per cent would still suffice. But in accepting this explanation, even provisionally, we had to face the improbability that a gas surrounding us on all sides, and present in enormous quantities, could have remained so long unsuspected.

The method of most universal application by which to test whether a gas is pure or a mixture of components of different densities is that of diffusion. By this means, Graham succeeded in effecting a partial separation of the nitrogen and oxygen of the air, in spite of the comparatively small difference of densities. If the atmosphere contain an unknown gas of anything like the density supposed, it should be possible to prove the fact by operations conducted upon air which had undergone atmolysis. This experiment, although in view from the first, was not executed until a later stage of the inquiry (§ VI), when results were obtained sufficient of themselves to prove that the atmosphere contains a previously unknown gas.

But although the method of diffusion was capable of deciding the main, or at any rate the first, question, it held out no prospect of isolating the new constituent of the atmosphere, and we therefore turned our attention in the first instance to the consideration of methods more strictly chemical. And here the question forced itself upon us as to what really was the evidence in favour of the prevalent doctrine that the inert residue from air after withdrawal of oxygen, water, and carbonic anhydride is all of one kind.

The identification of "phlogisticated air" with the constituent of nitric acid is due to Cavendish, whose method consisted in operating with electric sparks upon a short column of gas confined with potash over mercury at the upper end of an inverted U tube.[*]

Attempts to repeat Cavendish's experiment in Cavendish's

* "Experiments on Air," *Philosophical Transactions of the Royal Society* (London), Vol. 75 (1785), p. 372.

manner have only increased the admiration with which we regard this wonderful investigation. Working on almost micro-
scopical quantities of material, and by operations extending over
days and weeks, he thus established one of the most important
facts in chemistry. And what is still more to the purpose, he
raises as distinctly as we could do, and to a certain extent re-
solves, the question above suggested. The passage is so important
that it will be desirable to quote it at full length.

"As far as the experiments hitherto published extend, we
scarcely know more of the phlogisticated part of our atmosphere,
than that it is not diminished by lime-water, caustic alkalies, or
nitrous air; that it is unfit to support fire, or maintain life in animals; and that its specific gravity is not much less than that of
common air: so that though the nitrous acid, by being united to
phlogiston,* is converted into air possessed of these properties,
and consequently, though it was reasonable to suppose, that part
at least of the phlogisticated air of the atmosphere consists of this
acid united to phlogiston, yet it was fairly to be doubted whether
the whole is of this kind, or whether there are not in reality many
different substances compounded together by us under the name
of phlogisticated air. I therefore made an experiment to determine whether the whole of a given portion of the phlogisticated air of the atmosphere could be reduced to nitrous acid, or
whether there was not a part of a different nature to the rest,
which would refuse to undergo that change. The foregoing experiments indeed in some measure decided this point, as much
the greatest part of the air let up into the tube lost its elasticity;
yet as some remained unabsorbed it did not appear for certain
whether that was of the same nature as the rest or not. For this
purpose I diminished a similar mixture of dephlogisticated and
common air, in the same manner as before, till it was reduced to a
small part of its original bulk. I then, in order to decompound as
much as I could of the phlogisticated air which remained in the

* *I.e.*, deprived of oxygen. "Phlogisticated air" = nitrogen; "dephlogisticated air" = oxygen.

tube, added some dephlogisticated air to it, and continued the spark until no further diminution took place. Having by these means condensed as much as I could of the phlogisticated air, I let up some solution of liver of sulphur to absorb the dephlogisticated air; after which only a small bubble of air remained unabsorbed, which certainly was not more than $\frac{1}{120}$ of the bulk of the phlogisticated air let up into the tube; so that if there is any part of the phlogisticated air of our atmosphere which differs from the rest, and cannot be reduced to nitrous acid, we may safely conclude that it is not more than $\frac{1}{120}$th part of the whole."

Although Cavendish was satisfied with his result and does not decide whether the small residue was genuine, our experiments about to be related render it not improbable that his residue was really of a different kind from the main bulk of the "phlogisticated air" and contained the gas now called argon.

Cavendish gives data * from which it is possible to determine the rate of absorption of the mixed gases in his experiment. This was about 1 cc. per hour, of which two-fifths would be nitrogen.

Methods of Causing Free Nitrogen to Combine

To eliminate nitrogen from air, in order to ascertain whether any other gas could be detected, involves the use of some absorbent. The elements that have been found to combine directly with nitrogen are: boron, silicon, titanium, lithium, strontium, barium, magnesium, aluminium, mercury, and, under the influence of an electric discharge, hydrogen in presence of acid, and oxygen in presence of alkali. Besides these, a mixture of barium carbonate and carbon at a high temperature is known to be effective. Of those tried, magnesium in the form of turnings was found to be the best. When nitrogen is passed over magnesium heated in a tube of hard glass to bright redness, combustion with incandescence begins at the end of the tube through which the gas

* *Ibid.*, Vol. 78 (1788), p. 271.

is introduced and proceeds regularly until all the metal has been converted into nitride. Between 7 and 8 litres of nitrogen can be absorbed in a single tube; the nitride formed is a porous, dirty orange-coloured substance.

Early Experiments on Sparking Nitrogen with Oxygen in Presence of Alkali

In our earliest attempts to isolate the suspected gas by the method of Cavendish, we used a Ruhmkorff coil of medium size actuated by a battery of five Grove cells. The gases were contained in a test tube standing over a large quantity of weak alkali, and the current was conveyed in wires insulated by U-shaped glass tubes passing through the liquid round the mouth of the test tube. With the given battery and coil, a somewhat short spark or arc of about 5 mm. was found to be more favourable than a longer one. When the mixed gases were in the right proportion, the rate of absorption was about 30 cc. per hour, or thirty times as fast as Cavendish could work with the electrical machine of his day.

To take an example, one experiment of this kind started with 50 cc. of air. To this oxygen was gradually added until, oxygen being in excess, there was no perceptible contraction during an hour's sparking. The remaining gas was then transferred at the pneumatic trough to a small measuring vessel, sealed by mercury, in which the volume was found to be 1.0 cc. On treatment with alkaline pyrogallate, the gas shrank to 0.32 cc. That this small residue could not be nitrogen was argued from the fact that it had withstood the prolonged action of the spark, although mixed with oxygen in nearly the most favourable proportion.

The residue was then transferred to the test tube with an addition of another 50 cc. of air and the whole worked up with oxygen as before. The residue was now 2.2 cc., and, after removal of oxygen, 0.76 cc.

Although it seemed almost impossible that these residues could be either nitrogen or hydrogen, some anxiety was not unnatural, seeing that the final sparking took place under somewhat abnormal conditions. The space was very restricted, and the temperature (and with it the proportion of aqueous vapour) was unduly high. But any doubts that were felt upon this score were removed by comparison experiments in which the whole quantity of air operated on was very small. Thus, when a mixture of 5 cc. of air with 7 cc. of oxygen was sparked for $1\frac{1}{4}$ hours, the residue was 0.47 cc., and after removal of oxygen 0.06 cc. Several repetitions having given similar results, it became clear that the final residue did not depend upon anything that might happen when sparks passed through a greatly reduced volume, *but was in proportion to the amount of air operated upon.*

No satisfactory examination of the residue which refused to be oxidised could be made without the accumulation of a larger quantity. This, however, was difficult of attainment at the time in question. It was thought that the cause probably lay in the solubility of the gas in water, a suspicion since confirmed. At length, however, a sufficiency was collected to allow of sparking in a specially constructed tube, when a comparison with the air spectrum, taken under similar conditions, proved that, at any rate, the gas was not nitrogen. At first, scarcely a trace of the principal nitrogen lines could be seen, but after standing over water for an hour or two these lines became apparent.

Early Experiments on Withdrawal of Nitrogen from Air by Means of Red-hot Magnesium

A preliminary experiment carried out by Mr. Percy Williams on the absorption of atmospheric nitrogen, freed from oxygen by means of red-hot copper, in which the gas was not passed over, but simply allowed to remain in contact with the metal, gave a residue of density 14.88. This result, although not conclusive, was encouraging; and an attempt was made, on a larger scale, by passing atmospheric nitrogen backward and forward over red-hot magnesium from one large gas holder to another to obtain a considerable quantity of the heavier gas. In the course of ten days, about 1,500 cc. were collected and transferred gradually to a mercury gas holder, from which the gas was passed over soda-lime, phosphoric anhydride, magnesium at a red heat, copper oxide, soda-lime, and phosphoric anhydride into a second mercury gas holder. After some days, the gas was reduced in volume to about 200 cc., and its density was found to be 16.1. After further absorption, in which the volume was still further reduced, the density of the residue was increased to 19.09.

On passing sparks for several hours through a mixture of a small quantity of this gas with oxygen, its volume was still further reduced. Assuming that this reduction was due to the further elimination of nitrogen, the density of the remaining gas was calculated to be 20.0.

The spectrum of the gas of density 19.09, though showing nitrogen bands, showed many other lines that were not recognisable as belonging to any known element.

Proof of the Presence of Argon in Air by Means of Atmolysis

It has already (§ II) been suggested that if "atmospheric nitrogen" contains two gases of different densities, it should be possible to obtain direct evidence of the fact by the method of atmolysis. The present section contains an account of carefully conducted experiments directed to this end.

The atmolyser was prepared (after Graham) by combining a number of "churchwarden" tobacco pipes. At first, twelve pipes were used in three groups, each group including four pipes connected in series. The three groups were then connected in parallel and placed in a large glass tube closed in such a way that a partial vacuum could be maintained in the space outside the pipes by a water pump. One end of the combination of pipes was open to the atmosphere; the other end was connected to a bottle aspirator, initially full of water and so arranged as to draw about 2 per cent of the air which entered the other end of the pipes. The gas collected was thus a very small proportion of that which leaked through the pores of the pipes and should be relatively rich in the heavier constituents of the atmosphere. The flow of water from the aspirator could not be maintained very constant, but the rate of 2 per cent was never much exceeded.

The air thus obtained was treated exactly as ordinary air had been treated in determinations of the density of atmospheric nitrogen. Oxygen was removed by red-hot copper, followed by cupric oxide, ammonia by sulphuric acid, moisture and carbonic acid by potash and phosphoric anhydride.

In a total weight of approximately 2.3 g., the excess of weight of the diffused nitrogen over ordinary atmospheric nitrogen was, in four experiments, 0.0049, 0.0014, 0.0027, 0.0015.

The mean excess of the four determinations is 0.00262 g., or, if we omit the first, which depended upon a vacuum weighing of two months old, 0.00187 g.

The gas from prepared air was thus in every case denser than from unprepared air and to an extent much beyond the possible errors of experiment. The excess was, however, less than had been expected, and it was thought that the arrangement of the pipes could be improved. The final delivery of gas from each of the groups in parallel being so small in comparison with the whole streams concerned, it seemed possible that each group was not contributing its proper share and even that there might be a flow in the wrong direction at the delivery end of one or two of them. To meet this objection, the arrangement in parallel had to be abandoned, and for the remaining experiments eight pipes were connected in simple series. The porous surface in operation was thus reduced, but this was partly compensated for by an improved vacuum. Two experiments were made under the new conditions, in which the excess was I, 0.0037; II, 0.0033.

The excess being larger than before is doubtless due to the greater efficiency of the atmolysing apparatus. It should be mentioned that the above-recorded experiments include all that have been tried, and the conclusion seems inevitable that "atmospheric nitrogen" is a mixture, and not a simple body.

It was hoped that the concentration of the heavier constituent would be sufficient to facilitate its preparation in a pure state by the use of prepared air in substitution for ordinary air in the oxygen apparatus. The advance of 3½ mg. on the 11 mg. by which atmospheric nitrogen is heavier than chemical nitrogen is indeed not to be despised, and the use of prepared air would be convenient if the diffusion apparatus could be set up on a large scale and be made thoroughly self-acting.

Negative Experiments to Prove That Argon Is Not Derived from Nitrogen from Chemical Sources

Although the evidence of the existence of argon in the atmosphere, derived from the comparison of densities of atmospheric and chemical nitrogen and from the diffusion experiments (§ VI), appeared overwhelming, we have thought it undesirable to shrink from any labour that would tend to complete the verification. With this object in view, an experiment was undertaken and carried to a conclusion on November 13, in which 3 litres of chemical nitrogen, prepared from ammonium nitrite, were treated with oxygen in precisely the manner in which atmospheric nitrogen had been found to yield a residue of argon. The gas remaining at the close of the large-scale operations was worked up as usual with battery and coil until the spectrum showed only slight traces of the nitrogen lines. When cold, the residue measured 4 cc. This was transferred, and after treatment with alkaline pyrogallate to remove oxygen measured 3.3 cc. If atmospheric nitrogen had been employed, the final residue should have been about 30 cc. Of the 3.3 cc. actually left, a part is accounted for by an accident, and the result of the experiment is to show that argon is not formed by sparking a mixture of oxygen and chemical nitrogen.

In a second experiment of the same kind, 5,660 cc. of nitrogen from ammonium nitrite was treated with oxygen. The final residue was 3.5 cc. and was found to consist mainly of argon.

The source of the residual argon is to be sought in the water used for the manipulation of the large quantities of gas (6 litres of nitrogen and 11 litres of oxygen) employed. When carbonic acid was collected in a similar manner and subsequently absorbed by potash, it was found to have acquired a contamination consistent with this explanation.

Negative experiments were also carried out, absorbing nitrogen by means of magnesium. In one instance, 3 litres of nitrogen prepared from ammonium chloride and bleaching powder was reduced in volume to 4.5 cc., and on sparking with oxygen its volume was further reduced to about 3 cc. The residue appeared to consist of argon. Another experiment, in which 15 litres of nitrogen from ammonium nitrite was absorbed, gave a final residue of 3.5 cc. Atmospheric nitrogen, in the latter case, would have yielded 150 cc., hence less than $\frac{1}{40}$ of the normal quantity was obtained. It should be mentioned that leakage occurred at one stage, by which perhaps 200 cc. of air entered the apparatus; and, besides, the nitrogen was collected over water from which it doubtless acquired some argon. Quantitative negative experiments of this nature are exceedingly difficult and require a long time to carry them to a successful conclusion.

Separation of Argon on a Large Scale

To prepare argon on a large scale, air is freed from oxygen by means of red-hot copper. The residue is then passed from a gas holder through a combustion tube, heated in a furnace, and containing copper, in order to remove all traces of oxygen; the issuing gas is then dried by passage over soda-lime and phosphorus pentoxide, after passage through a small U tube containing sulphuric acid, to indicate the rate of flow. It then enters a combustion tube packed tightly with magnesium turnings and heated to redness in a second furnace. From this tube it passes through a second index tube and enters a small gas holder capable of containing 3 or 4 litres. A single tube of magnesium will absorb from 7 to 8 litres of nitrogen. The temperature must be nearly that of the fusion of the glass, and the current of gas must be carefully regulated, else the heat developed by the union of the magnesium with nitrogen will fuse the tube.

Having collected the residue from 100 or 150 litres of atmospheric nitrogen, which may amount to 4 or 5 litres, it is transferred to a small gas holder connected with an apparatus whereby, by means of a species of a self-acting Sprengel's pump, the gas is caused to circulate through a tube half filled with copper and half with copper oxide; it then traverses a tube half filled with soda-lime and half with phosphorus pentoxide; it then passes a reservoir of about 300 cc. capacity, from which, by raising a mercury reservoir, it can be expelled into a small gas holder. Next, it passes through a tube containing magnesium turnings heated to bright redness. The gas is thus freed from any possible contamination with oxygen, hydrogen, or hydrocarbons, and nitrogen is gradually absorbed. As the amount of gas in the tubes and reservoir diminishes in volume, it draws supplies from the gas holder, and finally the circulating system is full of argon in a pure state. The circulating system of tubes is connected with a mercury pump, so that, in changing the magnesium tube, no gas may be lost. Before ceasing to heat the magnesium tube, the system is pumped empty and the collected gas is restored to the gas holder; finally, all the argon is transferred from the mercury reservoir to the second small gas holder, which should preferably be filled with water saturated with argon, so as to prevent contamination from oxygen or nitrogen; or, if preferred, a mercury gas holder may be employed. The complete removal of nitrogen from argon is very slow toward the end, but circulation for a couple of days usually effects it.

The principal objection to the oxygen method of isolating argon, as hitherto described, is the extreme slowness of the operation. In extending the scale, we had the great advantage of the advice of Mr. Crookes, who not long since called attention to the flame rising from platinum terminals, which convey a high-tension alternating electric discharge, and pointed out its dependence upon combustion of the nitrogen and oxygen of the air.[*] The plant consists of a De Meritens alternator, actuated by a gas engine, and the currents are transformed to a high potential by means of a Ruhmkorff or other suitable induction coil. The highest rate of absorption of the mixed gases yet attained is 3 litres per hour, about 3,000 times that of Cavendish. It is necessary to keep the apparatus cool, and from this and other causes a good many difficulties have been encountered.

In one experiment of this kind, the total air led in after seven days' working amounted to 7,925 cc., and of oxygen (prepared from chlorate of potash), 9,137 cc. On the eighth and ninth days oxygen alone was added, of which about 500 cc. was consumed, while there remained about 700 cc. in the flask. Hence the proportion in which the air and oxygen combined was as 79 : 96. The progress of the removal of the nitrogen was examined from time to time with the spectroscope and became ultimately very slow. At last, the yellow line disappeared, the contraction having apparently stopped for two hours. It is worthy of notice that with the removal of the nitrogen, the arc discharge changes greatly in appearance, becoming narrower and blue rather than greenish in colour.

The final treatment of the residual 700 cc. of gas was on the model of the small-scale operations already described. Oxygen or hydrogen could be supplied at pleasure from an electrolytic apparatus, but in no way could the volume be reduced below 65 cc. This residue refused oxidation and showed no trace of the yellow line of nitrogen, even under favourable conditions.

When the gas stood for some days over water, the nitrogen line reasserted itself in the spectrum, and many hours' sparking with a little oxygen was required again to get rid of it. Intentional additions of air to gas free from nitrogen showed that about 1½

[*] *Chemical News*, Vol. 65 (1892), p. 301.

per cent was clearly, and about 3 per cent was conspicuously, visible. About the same numbers apply to the visibility of nitrogen in oxygen when sparked under these conditions, that is, at atmospheric pressure, and with a jar connected to the secondary terminals.

Density of Argon Prepared by Means of Oxygen

A first estimate of the density of argon prepared by the oxygen method was founded upon the data already recorded respecting the volume present in air, on the assumption that the accurately known densities of atmospheric and of chemical nitrogen differ on account of the presence of argon in the former and that during the treatment with oxygen nothing is oxidised except nitrogen. Thus, if

D = density of chemical nitrogen,
D′ = density of atmospheric nitrogen,
d = density of argon,
α = proportional volume of argon in atmospheric nitrogen,

the law of mixtures gives

$$\alpha d + (1 - \alpha)D = D',$$
or $\qquad d = D + (D' - D)/\alpha ,$

In this formula, D′ − D and α are both small, but they are known with fair accuracy. From the data already given

$$\alpha = \frac{65}{0.79 \times 7,925},$$

whence if (on an arbitrary scale of reckoning) D = 2.2990, D′ = 2.3102, we find $d = 3.378$. Thus if N_2 be 14, or O_2 be 16, the density of argon is 20.6.

A direct determination by weighing is desirable, but hitherto it has not been feasible to collect by this means sufficient to fill the large globe employed for other gases. A *mixture* of about 400 cc. of argon with pure oxygen, however, gave the weight 2.7315, 0.1045 in excess of the weight of oxygen, viz., 2.6270. Thus, if α be the ratio of the volume of argon to the whole volume, the number for argon will be

$$2.6270 + 0.1045/\alpha .$$

The value of α, being involved only in the excess of weight above that of oxygen, does not require to be known very accurately. Sufficiently concordant analyses by two methods gave $\alpha = 0.1845$; whence for the weight of the gas we get 3.193, so that, if $O_2 = 16$, the density of the gas would be 19.45. An allowance for residual nitrogen, still visible in the gas before admixture of oxygen, raises this number to 19.7, which may be taken as the density of pure argon resulting from this determination.

Density of Argon Prepared by Means of Magnesium

The density of the original sample of argon prepared has already been mentioned. It was 19.09; and, after sparking with oxygen, it was calculated to be 20.0. The most reliable results of a number of determinations give it as 19.90. The difficulty in accurately determining the density is to make sure that all nitrogen has been removed. The sample of density 19.90 showed no spectrum of nitrogen when examined in a vacuum tube. It is right, however, to remark that the highest density registered was 20.38. But there is some reason here to distrust the weighing of the vacuous globe.

Spectrum of Argon

The spectrum of argon, seen in a vacuum tube of about 3 mm. pressure, consists of a great number of lines, distributed over almost the whole visible field. Two lines are especially characteristic; they are less refrangible than the red lines of hydrogen or lithium and serve well to identify the gas, when examined in this way. Mr. Crookes, who will give a full account of the spectrum in a separate communication, has kindly furnished us with the accurate wave lengths of these lines, as well as of some others next to be described; they are respectively 696.56 and 705.64, 10^{-6} mm.

Besides these red lines, a bright yellow line, more refrangible than the sodium line, occurs at 603.84. A group of five bright-green lines occurs next, besides a number of less intensity. Of the group of five, the second, which is perhaps the most brilliant, has the wave length 561.00. There is next a blue or blue-violet line of wave length 470.2; and last, in the less easily visible part of the spectrum, there are five strong violet lines, of which the fourth, which is the most brilliant, has the wave length 420.0.

Unfortunately, the red lines, which are not to be mistaken for those of any other substance, are not easily seen when a jar discharge is passed through argon at atmospheric pressure, unless a large jar and a very powerful current be employed. The spectrum seen under these conditions has been examined by Professor Schuster. The most characteristic lines are perhaps those in the neighbourhood of F and are very easily seen if there be not too much nitrogen, in spite of the presence of some oxygen and water vapour. The approximate wave lengths are:

487.91	Strong.
[486.07]	F.
484.71	Not quite so strong.
480.52	Strong.
476.50	⎤
473.53	⎬ Fairly strong characteristic triplet.
472.56	⎦

It is necessary to anticipate Mr. Crookes's communication and to state that when the current is passed from the induction coil in one direction, that end of the capillary tube next the positive pole appears of a redder, and that next the negative pole of a bluer, hue. There are, in effect, two spectra, which Mr. Crookes has succeeded in separating to a considerable extent. Mr. E. C. C. Baly,* who has noticed a similar phenomenon, attributes it to the presence of two gases. He says: "When an electric current is passed through a mixture of two gases, one is separated from the other and appears in the negative glow." The conclusion would follow that what we have termed "argon" is in reality a mixture of two gases which have as yet not been separated. This conclusion, if true, is of great importance, and experiments are now in progress to test it by the use of other physical methods. The full bearing of this possibility will appear later.

The presence of a small quantity of nitrogen interferes greatly with the argon spectrum. But we have found that in a tube with platinum electrodes, after the discharge has been passed for four hours, the spectrum of nitrogen disappears, and the argon spectrum manifests itself in full purity. A specially constructed tube with magnesium electrodes, which we hoped would yield good results, removed all traces of nitrogen, it is true; but hydrogen was evolved from the magnesium and showed its characteristic lines very strongly. However, these are easily identified. The gas evolved on heating magnesium *in vacuo*, as proved by a separate experiment, consists entirely of hydrogen.

Mr. Crookes has established the identity of the chief lines of the spectrum of gas separated from air-nitrogen by aid of magnesium with that remaining after sparking the air-nitrogen with oxygen in presence of caustic soda solution.

Professor Schuster also has found the principal lines identical in the spectra of the two gases, as observed by the jar discharge at atmospheric pressure.

* Proceedings of the Physical Society (1893), p. 147.

Solubility of Argon in Water

Determinations of the solubility in water of argon, prepared by sparking, gave 3.94 volumes per 100 of water at 12°. The solubility of gas prepared by means of magnesium was found to be 4.05 volumes per 100 at 13.9°. The gas is therefore about 2½ times as soluble as nitrogen and possesses approximately the same solubility as oxygen.

The fact that argon is more soluble than nitrogen would lead us to expect it in increased proportion in the dissolved gases of rain water. Experiment has confirmed this anticipation. "Nitrogen" prepared from the dissolved gases of water supplied from a rain-water cistern was weighed upon two occasions. The weights, corresponding to those recorded in § 1, were 2.3221 and 2.3227, showing an excess of 24 mg. above the weight of true nitrogen. Since the corresponding excess for "atmospheric nitrogen" is 11 mg., we conclude that the water "nitrogen" is relatively more than twice as rich in argon.

On the other hand, gas evolved from the hot spring at Bath, and collected for us by Dr. A. Richardson, gave a residue after removal of oxygen and carbonic acid, whose weight was only about midway between that of true and atmospheric nitrogen.

Behaviour at Low Temperatures *

Preliminary experiments carried out to liquefy argon at a pressure of about 100 atmospheres and at a temperature of −90° failed. No appearance of liquefaction could be observed.

Professor Charles Olszewski, of Cracow, the well-known authority on the constants of liquefied gases at low temperatures, kindly offered to make experiments on the liquefaction of argon. His results are embodied in a separate communication, but it is

---

* The arrangements for the experiments upon this branch of the subject were left entirely in Professor Ramsay's hands.

allowable to state here that the gas has a lower critical temperature ($-121°$) and a lower boiling point ($-187°$) than oxygen and that he has succeeded in solidifying argon to white crystals, melting at $-189.6°$. The density of the liquid is approximately 1.5, that of oxygen being 1.124 and of nitrogen 0.885. The sample of gas he experimented with was exceptionally pure and had been prepared by help of magnesium. It showed no trace of nitrogen when examined in a vacuum tube.

Ratio of Specific Heats

In order to decide regarding the elementary or compound nature of argon, experiments were made on the velocity of sound in it. It will be remembered that, from the velocity of sound in a gas, the ratio of specific heat at constant pressure to that at constant volume can be deduced by means of the equation

$$n\lambda = v = \sqrt{\left\{\frac{e}{d}(1+\alpha t)\frac{C_p}{C_v}\right\}},$$

when n is the frequency, λ the wave length of sound, v its velocity, e the isothermal elasticity, d the density, $(1+\alpha t)$ the temperature correction, C_p the specific heat at constant pressure, and C_v that at constant volume. . . .

There can be no doubt, therefore, that argon gives practically the ratio of specific heats, viz., 1.66, proper to gas in which all the energy is translational. The only other gas that has been found to behave similarly is mercury gas, at a high temperature.[*]

Attempts to Induce Chemical Combination

Many attempts to induce argon to combine will be described in full in the complete paper. Suffice it to say here that all such

[*] Kundt and Warburg, *Poggendorff's Annalen der Physik*, Vol. 157 (1876), p. 353.

attempts have as yet proved abortive. Argon does not combine with oxygen in presence of alkali under the influence of the electric discharge, nor with hydrogen in presence of acid or alkali also when sparked; nor with chlorine, dry or moist, when sparked; nor with phosphorus at a bright-red heat, nor with sulphur at bright redness. Tellurium may be distilled in a current of the gas; so may sodium and potassium, their metallic lustre remaining unchanged. It is unabsorbed by passing it over fused red-hot caustic soda or soda-lime heated to bright redness; it passes unaffected over fused and bright red-hot potassium nitrate; and red-hot sodium peroxide does not combine with it. Persulphides of sodium and calcium are also without action at a red heat. Platinum black does not absorb it, nor does platinum sponge, and wet oxidising and chlorinating agents, such as nitrohydrochloric acid, bromine water, bromine and alkali, and hydrochloric acid and potassium permanganate, are entirely without action. Experiments with fluorine are in contemplation, but the difficulty is great; and an attempt will be made to produce a carbon arc in the gas. Mixtures of sodium and silica and of sodium and boracic anhydride are also without action; hence it appears to resist attack by nascent silicon and by nascent boron.

General Conclusions

It remains, finally, to discuss the probable nature of the gas, or mixture of gases, which we have succeeded in separating from atmospheric air and which has been provisionally named "argon."

The presence of argon in the atmosphere is proved by many lines of evidence. The higher density of "atmospheric nitrogen," and the uniformity in the density of samples of chemical nitrogen prepared from different compounds, lead to the conclusion that the cause of the anomaly is the presence of a heavy gas in air. If that gas possess the density 20 compared with hydrogen, "atmospheric nitrogen" should contain of it approximately 1 per cent. This is, in fact, found to be the case. Moreover, as nitrogen is removed from air by means of red-hot magnesium, the density of the remaining gas rises proportionately to the concentration of the heavier constituent.

Second. This gas has been concentrated in the atmosphere by diffusion. It is true that it cannot be freed from oxygen and nitrogen by diffusion, but the process of diffusion increases, relatively to nitrogen, the amount of argon in that portion which does not pass through the porous walls. This has been proved by its increase in density.

Third. As the solubility of argon in water is relatively high, it is to be expected that the density of the mixture of argon and nitrogen, pumped out of water along with oxygen, should, after the removal of the oxygen, exceed that of "atmospheric nitrogen." Experiment has shown that the density is considerably increased.

Fourth. It is in the highest degree improbable that two processes, so different from each other, should manufacture the same product. The explanation is simple if it be granted that these processes merely eliminate nitrogen from an atmospheric mixture. Moreover, if, as appears probable, argon be an element, or a mixture of elements, its manufacture would mean its separation from one of the substances employed. The gas which can be removed from red-hot magnesium in a vacuum has been found to be wholly hydrogen. Nitrogen from chemical sources has been practically all absorbed by magnesium and also when sparked in presence of oxygen; hence argon cannot have resulted from the decomposition of nitrogen. That it is not produced from oxygen is sufficiently borne out by its preparation by means of magnesium.

Other arguments could be adduced, but the above are sufficient to justify the conclusion that argon is present in the atmosphere.

The identity of the leading lines in the spectrum, the similar solubility, and the similar density appear to prove the identity of the argon prepared by both processes.

That argon is an element, or a mixture of elements, may be inferred from the observations of § XIV. For Clausius has shown that if K be the energy of translatory motion of the molecules of a gas, and H their whole kinetic energy, then

$$\frac{K}{H} = \frac{3(C_p - C_v)}{2C_v},$$

C_p and C_v denoting as usual the specific heat at constant pressure and at constant volume, respectively. Hence if, as for mercury vapour and for argon (§ XIV), the ratio of specific heats $C_p : C_v$ be $1\frac{2}{3}$, it follows that K = H, or that the whole kinetic energy of the gas is accounted for by the translatory motion of its molecules. In the case of mercury, the absence of interatomic energy is regarded as proof of the monatomic character of the vapour, and the conclusion holds equally good for argon.

The only alternative is to suppose that if argon molecules are di- or polyatomic, the atoms acquire no relative motion, even a rotation, a conclusion improbable in itself and one postulating the sphericity of such complex groups of atoms.

Now a monatomic gas can be only an element, or a mixture of elements; and hence it follows that argon is not of a compound nature.

From Avogadro's law, the density of a gas is half its molecular weight; and as the density of argon is approximately 20, hence its molecular weight must be 40. But its molecule is identical with its atom; hence its atomic weight, or, if it be a mixture, the mean of the atomic weights of that mixture, taken for the proportion in which they are present, must be 40.

There is evidence both for and against the hypothesis that argon is a mixture; for, owing to Mr. Crookes's observations of the dual character of its spectrum; against, because of Professor Olszewski's statement that it has a definite melting point, a definite boiling point, and a definite critical temperature and pressure; and because on compressing the gas in presence of its liquid, pressure remains sensibly constant until all gas has condensed to liquid. The latter experiments are the well-known criteria of a pure substance; the former is not known with certainty to be characteristic of a mixture. The conclusions which follow are, however, so startling that in our future experimental work we shall endeavour to decide the question by other means.

For the present, however, the balance of evidence seems to point to simplicity. We have therefore to discuss the relations to other elements of an element of atomic weight 40. We inclined for long to the view that argon was possibly one, or more than one, of the elements that might be expected to follow fluorine in the periodic classification of the elements—elements which should have an atomic weight between 19, that of fluorine, and 23, that of sodium. But this view is apparently put out of court by the discovery of the monatomic nature of its molecules.

The series of elements possessing atomic weights near 40 are:

Chlorine	35.5
Potassium	39.1
Calcium	40.0
Scandium	44.0

There can be no doubt that potassium, calcium, and scandium follow legitimately their predecessors in the vertical columns, lithium, beryllium, and boron, and that they are in almost certain relation with rubidium, strontium, and (but not so certainly) yttrium. If argon be a single element, then there is reason to doubt whether the periodic classification of the elements is complete—whether, in fact, elements may not exist which cannot be fitted among those of which it is composed. On the other hand, if argon be a mixture of two elements, they might find place in the eighth group, one after chlorine and one after bromine. Assuming 37 (the approximate mean between the atomic weights of chlorine and potassium) to be the atomic weight of the lighter element, and 40 the mean atomic weight found, and supposing that the second element has an atomic weight between those of bromine, 80, and rubidium, 85.5, viz., 82, the mixture should consist of 93.3 per cent of the lighter, and 6.7 per cent of the heavier, element. But it appears improbable that such a high percentage as 6.7 of a heavier element should have escaped detection during liquefaction.

If it be supposed that argon belongs to the eighth group, then its properties would fit fairly well with what might be anticipated. For the series, which contains

$$\mathrm{Si_{16}}^{IV}, \quad \mathrm{P_4}^{III\ and\ V}, \quad \mathrm{S}_{6\ to\ 2}^{II\ to\ VI}, \quad and\ \mathrm{Cl_2}^{I\ to\ VII},$$

might be expected to end with an element of monatomic molecules, of no valency, i.e., incapable of forming a compound, or if forming one, being an octad; and it would form a possible transition to potassium, with its monovalence, on the other hand. Such conceptions are, however, of a speculative nature; yet they may be perhaps excused if they in any way lead to experiments that tend to throw more light on the anomalies of this curious element.

In conclusion, it need excite no astonishment that argon is so indifferent to reagents. For mercury, although a monatomic element, forms compounds that are by no means stable at a high temperature in the gaseous state; and attempts to produce compounds of argon may be likened to attempts to cause combination between mercury gas at 800° and other elements. As for the physical condition of argon, that of a gas, we possess no knowledge why carbon, with its low atomic weight, should be a solid, while nitrogen is a gas, except insofar as we ascribe molecular complexity to the former and comparative molecular simplicity to the latter. Argon, with its comparatively low density and its molecular simplicity, might well be expected to rank among the gases. And its inertness, which has suggested its name, sufficiently explains why it has not previously been discovered as a constituent of compound bodies.

We would suggest for this element, assuming provisionally that it is not a mixture, the symbol A.

We have to record our thanks to Messrs. Gordon, Kellas, and Matthews, who have materially assisted us in the prosecution of this research.

7

THE PATH BRANCHES

As we have seen, the concept of atomic weight rested on the idea that matter consists of indivisible particles. By the turn of the century, little could yet be said about the actual size of these particles or their number in any visible and weighable portion of a substance. The original idea of Dalton was that the process of division always led to the same insurmountable limit, so far as physical analysis goes. Yet, on the assumption that chemical combinations between elements occur in simple proportions of their atoms, chemical analysis did permit the calculation of proportions of the weights of these intangible, elementary atoms. And when such proportions were expressed in terms of a selected standard of units—for example, by assigning the value 1 to the "atom" of hydrogen—atomic weights were calculable, provided it was known in what relative numbers the elements formed the compound.

Dulong and Petit had found one rule for determining such relative numbers by means of the atomic heat (1819); for gases, it was a great aid to have Avogadro's rule for the number of atoms that are combined as molecules. Thus a distinction was made between atomic weight and equivalent weight. For instance, one unit of hydrogen, say one gram, forms water with eight grams of oxygen. The equivalent weight of oxygen thus is found to be 8, but its atomic weight is twice this number.

An additional rule for determining equivalent weights had been developed by Michael Faraday (1791–1867) from his researches on electricity. In 1836 he wrote:

> The equivalent weights of bodies are simply those quantities of them which contain equal quantities of electricity. Or, if we adopt the atomic theory . . . the atoms of bodies which are equivalent to each other in their ordinary chemical actions have equal quantities of electricity associated with them. But I must confess I am jealous of the term *atom;* for though it is very easy to talk of atoms, it is very difficult to form a clear idea of their nature, especially when compound bodies are under consideration.

Faraday studied the electrolytic development of hydrogen and oxygen from water that was acidified by sulphuric acid for better electric conductivity. A few experiments with fused salts gave equivalents that were a little too high for tin, too low for lead. By a great intuition, Faraday expanded his few experiments into a general law of the electrochemical equivalence, which was proved correct fifty years later, in 1886, mainly by the work of the brothers Friedrich and Wilhelm Kohlrausch. Yet Faraday's electrical approach brought researchers no closer to an understanding of what the atom actually was.

Truly it was, in Faraday's words, "very difficult to form a clear idea" of atoms; nevertheless, the determination of atomic weights, in the restricted sense of combining proportions, remained an important task to which many chemists devoted themselves.

In time, the interest in atomic weights gradually became an independent pathway from the quest for an understanding of the nature of the atom. Moreover, the search for increased precision in this field similarly became separated from the task of checking the old hypothesis of William Prout that hydrogen was the real primary matter in all elements.

Theodore William Richards (1868–1928) became a traveler down the familiar path of research in atomic weights through the influence of his teacher, Josiah Parsons Cooke (1827–1894), at Harvard University. Since the method of calculating the atomic-weight relationships relied on a balance between chemically defined substances, the isolation of pure substances was most important. High standards in purity of substances and precision of analysis were goals that needed no further justification. They were pursued in many laboratories by both chemists and physicists. And while these goals had merits of their own, they were soon to become most important for the support of the startling new general theories of researchers seeking a more elusive path.

In the following excerpted passages, Richards surveys the branch of chemistry that wound still further into the province of atomic weight. He concludes:

Chemistry is still largely an inductive science; when we have discovered the realities, we shall be in a position to attempt to explain them. In the meantime, more accurate values, discovered little by little through patient investigation, will be of use to the thousands of men throughout the world who daily employ these fundamental data of chemistry.

And, as we shall soon see, "these fundamental data," relating to atomic weights, were of crucial value to the greatest adventure in modern science: the road that began with the discovery of radioactivity.

◆

Atomic Weights [1]

THEODORE W. RICHARDS

. . . Although details must be omitted, a sketch of my work may nevertheless be of interest. The first problem that I undertook, more than a quarter of a century ago, was the determination of the ratio between oxygen and hydrogen, under the guidance of Cooke. We weighed the hydrogen directly in large glass globes and, after having burnt it with copper oxide, determined the weight of water formed. The outcome, when all corrections had been applied, gave a result for hydrogen only 0.0004 different from the value 1.0078 now generally accepted. . . .

During the work on oxygen and hydrogen, it was necessary to study very carefully the preparation of the oxide of copper, which was found to exhibit so many peculiarities as to cause doubt concerning the accepted atomic weight of copper, partly derived from the analysis of the oxide. Thus began a research that lasted four years and involved the study of many methods and many compounds of copper.

It was proved conclusively that the copper oxide that had been previously used for determining the exact ratio of copper to oxygen must have contained included gases. Thus it contained less copper than the pure compound, and the atomic weight of the element appeared to be lower than the true value.

Besides applying this correction to the older result, entirely new methods were used. The relation of copper to silver, of copper to bromine, and of copper to sulphuric acid were all determined with care, and all yielded essentially the same new value, thus leaving no doubt that the old value for copper was nearly half a per cent too low.

[1] Excerpts from an address presented before the Chicago Section of the American Chemical Society on the occasion of the award of the Willard Gibbs Medal, May 17, 1912. *Journal of the American Chemistry Society*, Vol. 34 (1912), 959–971.

The next element to be investigated was barium, to which attention had been called because of certain anomalies in an attempt to find the ratio between barium and copper sulphates in the previous research. Both barium chloride and barium bromide were analyzed, taking great care to drive off all water without decomposing the salts. Much time was spent upon the preparation of pure silver, and every step of the analysis was tested, taking great heed especially of the solubility of silver chloride. The result showed that barium was previously almost as inexact as copper, the new value being about 0.3 of a unit higher than the old one. In this case, as in the other, not only were the new results obtained but also the reasons for the deviations in the old ones were made clear.

Next among the atomic weights, strontium was undertaken because of a suspicion that the same errors vitiating previous work on barium were also at work here. Moreover, I wished especially to obtain accurate values for those elements that form well-marked series in the periodic system, because among such elements it seems reasonable to suppose that a possible numerical relation is most likely to be found. The salts used were the same as those employed for barium, namely the chloride and bromide, but distinct improvements in manipulation were introduced. In this work on strontium, the earliest forms of the so-called "bottling apparatus" were used, and also the nephelometer—the first being a device for drying hygroscopic salts without contact with the moisture of the air, and the second being an instrument that made possible the detection of faint traces of precipitate suspended in liquids. A puzzling outcome of this research lay in the fact that the results from the chloride and the bromide did not seem to be exactly alike; they differed by an amount too great to be ascribed to the probable error in analysis. The reason for this was found nearly ten years afterward in the discovery that the error lay not in the results for strontium but rather in the accepted value of the atomic weight of chlorine. . . .

[Now Richards describes a method to avert contamination prior to weighing.]

The simple device consists of a hard-glass or quartz ignition tube fitted to a soft-glass tube which has a projection or pocket in one side. A weighing bottle is placed at the end of the latter tube, and its stopper in the pocket. The boat containing the substance to be dried is heated in the ignition tube, surrounded by an atmosphere consisting of any desired mixture of gases. These gases are displaced, after partial cooling, first by nitrogen, and then by pure dry air, and the boat is pushed past the stopper into the weighing bottle, the stopper being then forced into place, and the substance thus shut up in an entirely dry atmosphere. The weighing bottle may now be removed, placed in an ordinary desiccator, and weighed at leisure. The substance is really dry, and its weight has definite significance.*

Nickel, cobalt, and iron, attacked with the help of Allerton Cushman and Gregory P. Baxter, formed the next subjects of investigation, each metal bringing its own new problem. It was conclusively proved that nickel and cobalt really have different atomic weights and that the value for iron is much lower than it had been supposed to be.

Simultaneously with this work, another of quite a different nature was in progress. The question as to whether the chemical combining proportions agree exactly with the electrolytic equivalents was one that had never been satisfactorily settled. According to the atomic hypothesis, there was every reason to believe that they should precisely agree, but the matter was one that could not be settled without actual experiment. The electrochemical equivalent offers an entirely new method of approach with regard to the combining proportions. . . . I sought, with the efficient help of E. Collins and G. W. Heimrod, to compare the weight of silver and copper precipitated from their salts by an identical current.

Later the precipitation of silver was studied in much more detail under varying circumstances, and the former results were confirmed and amplified.† With the help of W. N. Stull, it was

* Faraday lecture, *Science*, N. S., Vol. 34, Oct. 27 (1911), pp. 537–550.
† *Proceedings of the American Academy*, Vol. 37 (1902), p. 415.

shown also that precisely the same quantity of silver is precipitated from a solution of silver nitrate in fused sodium and potassium nitrates at 250° as from an aqueous solution at 20°, when the proper correction has been made for traces of solvent included in the crystals.* This is perhaps the most striking combination of the exact and universal precision of Faraday's law that has ever been offered.

Thus the atomic weights are shown to represent numerical relations that persist under widely differing conditions.

. . . Curiosity concerning uranium was heightened by Becquerel's and the Curies' brilliant discoveries and by the recent disintegration theory which imagines that uranium and radium are merely aggregates that may be called "elemental compounds" of helium with lead. Ramsay has emphasized the fact that the atomic weights alone of these elements are capable of finally solving the puzzle.

Radium has recently been determined with great precision by Hönigschmid at Vienna, using the Harvard methods, learned during the study of its analogue calcium, and found to be 225.95. If uranium should be found to be 237.83—different from radium by just three times the atomic weight of helium—the theory concerning the relation of the two so-called elements would receive substantial support. Hence, a systematic and searching repetition of the early careful Harvard work on uranium of B. S. Merigold is now in progress in Cambridge; and with the help of quartz tubes and other modern appliances, we hope to obtain more conclusive results either for or against the hypothesis. Incidentally, it may be said that the old Harvard work pointed to the value of 238.4, a quantity over half a unit higher than the value demanded by the disintegration theory. Thus, a physicochemical problem demanding great purity of material led to a quantitative research of unexpected magnitude; and in turn this quantitative investigation depended continually upon physicochemical methods and considerations, many of them having been acquired since the days of Stas. There is not time to go into the details tonight

* Ibid., Vol. 38 (1902), p. 409.

either of our new precautions or the errors into which Stas had unwittingly fallen, but the outcome was that common salt prepared in the state of great purity was found to yield the same low atomic weight of sodium as the pure bromide; and simultaneously Stas's atomic weight of chlorine as referred to silver was found to be appreciably too low. Turning back now to strontium, where I had previously found a discrepancy between the chloride and the bromide, it appeared, as I have already said, that this had been due to the erroneous value for chlorine; with the new value, the result from the chloride agreed with that from the bromide. Other elements also into which chlorine entered needed correction, but fortunately these were very few in number, because we had intentionally almost always employed the bromide on account of its greater analytical certainty. Moreover, metals with high equivalents are affected less by the error in chlorine than those like sodium with low equivalents.

The discovery of error in two of Stas's most accurately determined results led to a natural suspicion that the others also needed revision. Accordingly, redeterminations of potassium with the help of A. Staehler and E. Mueller, of sulphur with that of Grinnell Jones, and of nitrogen, first with the help of G. S. Forbes, and finally in collaboration with Köthner and Tiede during my term of service at the University of Berlin, were undertaken. Potassium chloride and bromide were both analyzed with all the care used in the case of sodium; sulphur was approached by a new method involving the conversion of silver sulphate into the chloride; and nitrogen was attacked both by the synthesis of silver nitrate and by the analysis of ammonium chloride. In each case, Stas's results were found to be somewhat in error. The work on silver nitrate was in some ways the most convincing of all, because in this case it was possible to prove that the salt was essentially free from water by decomposing it and passing the products of decomposition, suitably treated, through a phosphorus pentoxide tube. No more concordant results have ever been secured in the Harvard Laboratory than the six successive experiments by which the silver was converted into silver nitrate—the extreme variation between the results being less than one-thousandth of a per cent. If any error existed in them, it was an error of amazing constancy.

If I were to sum up in a few words the lessons of these protracted investigations, I should be inclined to say that the secret of success in the study of atomic weights lies in carefully choosing the particular substances and processes employed and in checking every operation by parallel experiments so that every unknown chemical and physical error will gradually be ferreted out of its hiding place. The most important causes of inaccuracy are the solubility of precipitates and of the material of containing vessels, the occlusion of foreign substances by solids, and especially the presence of retaining moisture in almost everything. Each of these disturbing circumstances varies with each individual case. Far more depends upon the intelligent choice of the conditions of experiment than upon the mere mechanical execution of the operations, although that, too, is important. I have often quoted the innocent remark that has occasionally been made to me: "What wonderfully fine scales you must have to weigh atoms!" Tonight I have endeavored to point out that the purely chemical work, which precedes the introduction of the substance into the balance case, is far more important than the mere operation of weighing. Moreover, speculation and the higher mathematics are as yet of little service to us in this quest; I cannot help thinking that any ultimate general conclusion must rest upon careful laboratory work. Chemistry is still largely an inductive science; when we have discovered the realities, we shall be in a position to attempt to explain them. In the meantime, more accurate values, discovered little by little through patient investigation, will be of use to the thousands of men throughout the world who daily employ these fundamental data of chemistry.

◆

In the foregoing work purity is the central theme for Richards. The purity of a chemical substance is assaulted by influences from its surroundings. Richards had to consider at least three such influences: 1. the medium from which the substance is separated in insoluble form, as in the precipitation of silver chloride from water; 2. the contact with the material used as a container; 3. the exposure to the air and moisture in which we perform the experiment. We arrive at precision for atomic weights of the elements only to the degree at which we achieve purity. To do that, we must exclude, or at least modify, "natural" surroundings. In this respect, chemical purity appears to be "unnatural," ideal, while being aimed at that deeper "reality" that does not show on the surface.

In the concept of purity the ideal part is our human intuition. The same kind of intuition was the basis of speculations about the existence of atoms and about a primordial substance in all matter. The advances on the path of science lead to increasingly complicated means and methods of exploring nature, but they only seemed to lead away from the human intuition. This is particularly evident in the following adventure in chemistry.

An understanding of F. W. Aston's work requires some added background. Chemists of the seventeenth century had called themselves "philosophers by fire" because by the heat of fire they achieved their analyses and syntheses. Chemists of the late eighteenth century had introduced the use of electricity as an additional tool. The spark of electricity passing the gap between two wires served to combine hydrogen or nitrogen with oxygen or to separate ammonia, NH_3, into nitrogen and hydrogen. Electricity, passing through liquids, enabled Humphry Davy to obtain sodium, potassium, and calcium from their salts. Davy also experimented with passing electricity through gases. In 1821, he produced an arc between charcoal points and found that he could extend this arc over a distance of 7 inches in a vacuum. As his source of electricity, he used the 2,000-cell voltaic battery of the Royal Institution.

Research with electricity and its effect on gases was to play an enormous role in the investigation of atomic structure toward the end of the nineteenth and first part of the twentieth centuries, the revolutionary period that ushered in the present age in chemistry and physics. Researchers found that the low pressure of a gas facilitates the passage of electricity. At the very low pressures Heinrich Geissler (1814–1879) achieved in glass tubes of his construction by means of his mercury vapor pump, extraordinary new phenomena were noted. A glow spread from the cathode, the metal connected with the negative pole of the battery. Obstacles placed in the path of this glow cast a shadow.

In 1876, Eugen Goldstein (1850–1930) concluded that the light from the cathode proceeded in straight lines; they were named cathode rays. Since these rays started from the negative pole, it seemed likely to William Crookes that they carried a negative charge. If this were so, a cathode ray should correspond to a wire conducting electricity. As Faraday had found, such a wire is moved when a magnetic field is applied. Crookes put a plate with a narrow slit between cathode and anode so as to produce a narrow beam. When he brought the discharge tube between the poles of a magnet, he saw the beam deflected in accordance with Faraday's rule. This confirmed the assumption that the beam consisted of negative particles.

At that time, an electric current was considered as the flow of negative particles in one direction and of positive particles in the other. Where was this opposite flow in the discharge tube? Thinking that perhaps the positive particles could not go through a solid cathode, Goldstein used a perforated cathode. The result was striking: luminous rays started from the cathode in the direction away from the anode. They appeared yellow when the tube contained air, rose when it contained hydrogen. They were also deflected through a magnetic field, but in a direction which characterized them as positive rays.

A ray here means a stream of electrically charged particles. The complete description therefore requires a knowledge of velocity, electric charge, and mass, symbolized by v, e, and m. For the negative rays, Joseph John Thomson (1856–1940) measured v by applying to a ray a magnetic and an electrostatic field. The magnetic field was arranged so that it would deflect the ray upward, the electrostatic field so as to turn the ray downward. At a certain ratio of the strengths of the two fields, their influences canceled each other; this ratio corresponds with the velocity, v. The application of a magnetic field alone produced a curvature of the path from which the ratio e/m followed when the velocity was known. This picture was completed when a method for measuring e was developed.

Cathode rays appeared to consist of "corpuscles," as Thomson called what were later named "electrons." They were of very small mass and very large electrical charge, moving at high speeds, which under certain conditions could approach the velocity of light.

In Thomson's view, these corpuscles were torn out of the atoms or molecules of the gas by the action of the cathode ray. Such robbery left a positively charged residue consisting of the atom or molecule deprived of one, or sometimes two, electrons. Thomson knew that under the influence of simultaneously applied magnetic and electrostatic fields, all particles having the same mass and charge, but different velocities, will hit a target in the form of a parabola. Particles of the same mass, differing in charge as well as velocity, will form a family of parabolas, each parabola containing particles of the same charge. Rays composed of different masses of particles are spread out into a mass spectrum of parabolas. The measurement of positive rays produced by the passage of electricity through gases at very low pressure thus became a method for determining atomic weights of the gases from which the particles were expelled.

J. J. Thomson completed the first mass spectrograph in 1912. Shortly afterward, this instrument provided answers to an intriguing problem. In January, 1913, Kasimir Fajans announced that each of the end products in the three radioactive decay series—uranium, radium, and thorium—behaved chemically like lead. Moreover, none of these end products could be separated, although their atomic weights most certainly should have been different.

A month later, Frederick Soddy (1877–1956) published similar findings and concluded that these products of radioactive decay belonged to the same place in the periodic system; he proposed to call them "isotopes," from the Greek word for "the same place." Soddy must have chosen this classical reference because his special discovery could be expected to indicate a more general rule, one that applied as well to elements that were not radioactive. Certainly isotopes could exist outside the radioactive group, but they would always go chemically undetected because the several isotopes of an element behaved as one and the same in all chemical tests. Identification of the isotopes would therefore require methods that were sensitive to differences in mass, rather than chemistry. For a long time, science had relied considerably on chemical analysis to assign atomic weights, working with the relative combining proportions of the elements. Hence Thomson's mass spectrograph was called upon to determine mass differences and atomic weights in atoms that were the same in their chemical reactivity.

Thomson's work at Trinity College, Cambridge, was based on the ability to combine mathematical ingenuity with skill in experimenting and a prowess in constructing delicate apparatus. Francis William Aston (1877–1945), who joined Thomson in 1909, also had this ability to a high degree. Difficult experiments and calculations led to results that seemed to confirm the ideas of William Prout. First neon, and somewhat later chlorine, appeared to consist of isotopes with atomic weights that are simple multiples of the atomic weight of hydrogen.

Like the photospectrometer of Kirchhoff and Bunsen, the mass spectrometer of Thomson and Aston has been developed into an instrument that is widely used today in science and industry.

◆

The Constitution of Atmospheric Neon [2]

FREDERICK WILLIAM ASTON

In 1898, neon was isolated from the atmosphere, in which it occurs to the extent of .00123 per cent, by volume, by Ramsay and Travers, and was accepted as an elementary monatomic gas of the helium group. Its density was measured with extreme care by Watson [*] and found to correspond with an atomic weight 20.200 (O = 16), making it the lightest element to diverge from the whole-number rule in an unmistakable manner.

Neon has many very remarkable properties: its compressibility, viscosity, and dielectric cohesion are all abnormal; but the first suggestion that it might be a mixture was the observation in 1912 by Sir J. J. Thomson of a faint but unmistakable parabola at a position corresponding roughly to an atomic weight 22, in addition to the expected one at 20, in positive-ray photographs, whenever neon was present in the discharge bulb. The first plate which showed this was obtained from a sample of the lighter constituents of air supplied by Sir James Dewar; other specimens of impure neon gave a similar result. So also did a portion of the gas used by Watson in the atomic-weight determinations, which fact, together with the complete invisibility of any parabola at 22 on hundreds of plates where neon was known to be absent, was very strong evidence that the line was ascribable to neon and to neon alone.

These facts led the author to undertake a searching investigation on the constitution of the gas by two distinct lines of attack; first, attempts at separation; secondly, accumulation of the evidence obtainable by positive rays.

In periodic tables of the elements arranged in order of their

[2] Abridged from *Philosophical Magazine*, Ser. 6, Vol. 39, No. 232 (April, 1920).
[*] *Journal of the Chemical Society Transactions*, Vol. 1 (1910), p. 810.

atomic weights, the part lying between fluorine on the one hand and sodium on the other is of considerable interest.

Soon after the discovery of argon, and while the monatomic nature of its molecule was still under discussion, Emerson Reynolds, in a letter to *Nature* (March 21, 1895), described a particular periodic diagram which he had used with advantage. In this letter, referring to the occurrence of the groups Fe, Ni, Co; Ru, Rh, Pd; and Os, Ir, Pt; the following passage occurs:

". . . the distribution of the triplets throughout the whole of the best-known elements is so nearly regular that it is difficult to avoid the inference that three elements should also be found in the symmetrical position between 19 and 23,[3] i.e., between F and Na, . . . of which argon may be one. . . ."

Intensity of the Parabolas The relative intensity of the Ne^α and Ne^β parabolas obtained from atmospheric neon untreated by diffusion has been estimated by three different observers as about ten to one. Its apparent invariability is corroborative evidence against the possibility of the 22 line being due to the presence of other gases in the discharge bulb.

It will be seen that although by Thomson's system of analysis the presence of two isotopes in atmospheric neon was indicated by several lines of reasoning, none of them can be regarded as quite conclusive, and it was realized that, failing separation, the most satisfactory proof would be afforded by measurements of atomic weight so accurate as to prove beyond dispute that neither constituent corresponded with the accepted atomic weight of atmospheric neon.

Evidence of the Positive-ray Spectrograph

The "mass spectra" yielded by the new method of positive-ray analysis recently described * supply these measurements in an entirely satisfactory manner. . . . They are important lines of

---

[3] Position by atomic weight in the periodic table.
* F. W. Aston, *Philosophical Magazine*, December, 1919.

reference and are certainly of the relative masses given above to the order of accuracy (one-tenth per cent) claimed in the present experiment.

In A IV. the deflexion has been still further increased, and a new group of lines, the C_2 Group 24, 25, 26, 27, 28, 29, 30, containing the strong reference line of CO (or C_2H_4), have come into view.[4] In A III. of the C_1 group, only 15 and 16 are visible, and in A V. the C_2 group has moved to the left and the strong line 44, CO_2 is seen to the right.

Plate B was taken with CO to which about 20 per cent of atmospheric neon had been added. Considering the spectrum B III., it will be seen that four unmistakably new lines have made their appearance, one pair between the C_1 and C_2 groups, another weaker pair to the left of the C_1 group. The first pair are $(Ne^{\alpha})+$ 20 and $(Ne^{\beta})+$ 22 singly charged; the second pair are the same atoms with double charges $10(Ne^{\alpha})++$ and $11 (Ne^{\beta})++$ respectively. The other spectra consist of lines already mentioned brought into different positions to increase the convenience and accuracy of comparison, and, in addition, there are on C I. two other valuable reference lines, O^{++} apparent mass 8, and on the extreme left just visible C^{++} apparent mass 6.

Method of Comparing Masses

It will be noticed that although the lines are broad (the best focus was only obtained by a series of trials after these results were completed), their edges—particularly their left-hand edges —are remarkably sharp, so that measurements of a reasonably good line from the register spot repeat to a twentieth of a milli-metre with certainty. Hence, for accurate determination of un-known lines, only two assumptions need be made: first, that the masses of the reference lines are known; and secondly, that, what-ever the function connecting displacement with mass, any two

---

[4] Examine the sample of an Aston mass spectrograph that appears further on in this selection. (Ed.)

positions on the spectrum being taken, the *ratio* of any two masses giving lines in these positions will be constant. This being so, by moving a group of reference lines into overlapping positions along the spectrum it is clear that the whole length can be plotted out and calibrated.

Fortunately there is an easy method of testing both these assumptions, for although it is impossible to measure the magnetic field to one-tenth per cent, it can be kept constant to that accuracy while the electric field is altered by a known ratio. . . . To take a typical case, the position occupied by carbon, with a field of 320 volts, should be exactly coincident with the position occupied by oxygen, with 240 volts, when the magnetic field is constant. Over the range of fields used in the case of neon, all such coincidences when expected have been found to occur within the error of experiment, whatever the position on the plate.

For some reason, by no means obvious, connected with the geometry of the apparatus, the relation between displacement and mass is very nearly linear, a fact which lightens the labour and increases the accuracy of calibration very considerably.

. . . The above figures therefore can be accepted as fairly conclusive evidence that atmospheric neon contains two isotopes of atomic weights 20.00 and 22.00, respectively, to an accuracy of about one-tenth per cent.

In order to give the accepted density, the quantities required are 90 per cent and 10 per cent, which is in good agreement with the estimated intensity of the lines.

Possibility of a Third Isotope

On the clearest spectra obtained with neon, there are distinct indications of a line corresponding to an isotope of mass 21. This line is extremely faint, so that if this constituent exists, its proportion would be very small, probably well under 1 per cent, and it would not affect the density appreciably. Attempts to bring this line out more distinctly by longer exposures have not succeeded, owing to the fogging from the strong neighbouring lines, but it is intended to return to this point when further improvements of the method give hope of more conclusive results.

The Discharge Tube

Figure 7–1 is a rough diagram of the present arrangement. The discharge tube B is an ordinary X-ray bulb 20 cm. in diameter. The anode A is of aluminium wire 3 mm. thick surrounded concentrically by an insulated aluminium tube 7 mm. wide to protect the glass walls, as in the Lodge valve.

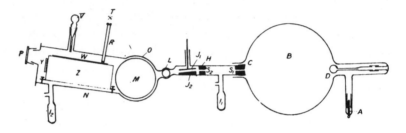

Figure 7–1.

The aluminium cathode C, 2.5 cm. wide, is concave, about 8 cm. radius of curvature, and is placed just in the neck of the bulb—this shape and position having been adopted after a short preliminary research. In order to protect the opposite end of the bulb, which would be immediately melted by the very concentrated beam of cathode rays, a silica bulb D about 12 mm. diameter is mounted as indicated. The use of silica as an anticathode was suggested by Professor Lindemann and has the great advantage of cutting down the production of undesirable X rays to a minimum.

The discharge is maintained by means of a large induction coil actuated by a mercury coal-gas break. . . .

The method of mounting the cathode will be readily seen from Figure 7–2, which shows part of the apparatus in greater detail.

The neck of the bulb is ground off short and cemented with wax to the flat brass collar E, which forms the mouth of an annular space between a wide outer tube F and the inner tube carrying the cathode. The concentric position of the neck is assured by three small ears of brass not shown. The wax joint is kept cool by circulating water through the copper pipe shown in section at G.

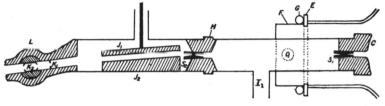

Figure 7–2.

The gas to be analysed is admitted from the customary fine leak into the annular space and so to the discharge by means of the side tube attached to F shown in dotted section at Q. Exhaustion is performed by a Gaede mercury pump through a similar tube on the opposite side. The reason for this arrangement is that the space behind the cathode is the only part of the discharge bulb in which the gas is not raised to an extremely high potential. If the inlet or outlet is anywhere in front of the cathode, failing special guards, the discharge is certain to strike to the pump or the gas reservoir. Such special guards have been made in the past by means of dummy cathodes in the bore of the tubes, but, notwithstanding the fact that the gas can only reach the bulb by diffusion, the present arrangement is far more satisfactory and has the additional advantage of enabling the bulb to be dismounted by breaking one joint only.

The Slit System

The centre of the cathode is pierced with a 3 mm. hole, the back of which is coned out to fit one of the standard slits S_1. The back of the cathode is turned a gastight fit in the brass tube 2 cm. diameter carrying it, the other end of which bears the brass plug H, which is also coned and fitted with the second slit S_2. The two slits, which are .05 mm. wide by 2 mm. long, can be accurately adjusted parallel by means of their diffraction patterns. The space between the slits, which are about 10 cm. apart, is kept exhausted to the highest degree by the charcoal tube I_1. By this arrangement it will be seen that not only is loss of rays by collision and neutralization reduced to a minimum, but any serious leak of gas from the bulb to the camera is eliminated altogether.

The Electric Field

The spreading of the heterogeneous ribbon of rays formed by the slits into an electric spectrum takes place between two parallel flat brass surfaces, J_1, J_2, 5 cm. long, held 2.8 mm. apart by glass distance pieces, the whole system being wedged immovably in the brass containing tube in the position shown. The lower surface is cut from a solid cylinder fitting the tube and connected to it and earth.[5] The upper surface is a thick brass plate, which can be raised to the desired potential by means of a set of small storage cells. In order to have the plates as near together as possible, they are sloped at 1 in 20—i.e., half the angle of slope of the mean ray of the part of the spectrum which is to be selected by the diaphragms. Of these there are two: one, K_1, an oblong aperture in a clean brass plate, is fixed just in front of the second movable one, K_2, which is mounted in the bore of a carefully ground stopcock L. The function of the first diaphragm is to prevent any possibility of charged rays striking the greasy surface of the plug of the stopcock when the latter is in any working position. The variable diaphragm is in effect two square apertures sliding past each other as the plug of the stopcock is turned, the fact that they are not in the same plane being irrelevant.

[5] Electrical ground.

When the stopcock is fully open as sketched in Figure 7–2, the angle of rays passing is a maximum and may be stopped down to any desired extent by rotation of the plug, becoming zero before any greasy surface is exposed to the rays. Incidentally, the stopcock serves another and very convenient use, which is to cut off the camera from the discharge tube so that the latter need not be filled with air each time the former is opened to change the plate.

The Magnetic Field

After leaving the diaphragms, the rays pass between the pole pieces M of a large Du Bois magnet of 2,500 turns. The faces of these are circular, 8 cm. diameter, and held 3 mm. apart by brass distance pieces. The cylindrical pole pieces themselves are soldered into a brass tube O, which forms part of the camera N. When the latter is built into position, the pole pieces are drawn by screwed bolts into the arms of the magnet and so form a structure of great weight and rigidity and provide an admirable foundation for the whole apparatus. Current for the magnet is provided by a special set of large accumulators. The hydrogen lines are brought onto the plate at about 0.2 ampere, and an increase to 5 amperes, which gives practical saturation, only just brings the singly charged mercury lines into view. The discharge is protected from the strong field of the magnet by the usual soft-iron plates, not shown.

The Camera   The main body of the camera N is made of stout brass tube 6.4 cm. diameter, shaped to fit on to the transverse tube O containing the pole pieces. The construction of the plate holder is indicated by the side view in Figure 7–1 and an end-on view in Figure 7–3. The rays, after being magnetically deflected, pass between two vertical plates Z–Z about 3 mm. apart and finally reach the photographic plate through a narrow slot 2 mm. wide, 11.8 cm. long, cut in the horizontal metal plate X–X. The three

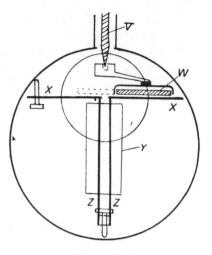

Figure 7–3.

brass plates forming a T-shaped girder are adjusted and locked in position by a set of three levelling screws at each end; the right-hand upper one is omitted in Figure 7–3. The plates Z–Z serve to protect the rays completely from any stray electric field, even that caused by the photographic plate itself becoming charged, until within a few millimetres of their point of impact.

The photographic plate W, which is a 2 cm. strip cut lengthwise from a 5 × 4 plate, is supported at its ends on two narrow transverse rails which raise it just clear of the plate X–X. Normally it lies to the right of the slot as indicated, and to make an exposure it is moved parallel to itself over the slot by means of a sort of double lazy tongs carrying wire claws which bracket the ends of the plate as shown. This mechanism, which is not shown in detail, is operated by means of a torque rod V working through a ground glass joint. Y is a small willemite screen.

The adjustment of the plate holder so that the sensitized surface should be at the best focal plane was done by taking a series of exposures of the bright hydrogen lines with different magnetic fields on a large plate placed in the empty camera at a small inclination to the vertical. On developing this, the actual track of the rays could be seen and the locus of points of maximum concentration determined. The final adjustment was made by trial and error and was exceedingly tedious, as air had to be admitted and a new plate inserted after each tentative small alteration of the levelling screws.

Experimental Procedure. The plate having been dried in a high vacuum overnight, the whole apparatus is exhausted as completely as possible by the pump with the stopcock L open. I_1 and I_2 are then cut off from the pump by stopcocks and immersed in liquid air for an hour or so. The electric field, which may range from 200 to 500 volts, is then applied and a small current passed through the magnet sufficient to bring the bright hydrogen molecule spot onto the willemite screen Y, where it can be inspected through the plate-glass back of the cap P. In the meantime, the leak, pump, and coil have all been started to get the bulb into the desired state.

As soon as this is obtained and has become steady, J_1 is earthed [6] to prevent any rays reaching the camera when the plate is moved over the slot to its first position, which is judged by inspection through P with a nonactinic lamp. The magnet current having been set to the particular value desired and the diaphragm adjusted, the coil is momentarily interrupted while J_1 is raised to the desired potential, after which the exposure starts. During this, preferably both at the beginning and the end, light from a lamp T is admitted for a few seconds down the tube R (Figure 7–1), the ends of which are pierced with two tiny circular holes. The lower hole is very close to the plate, so that a circular dot or register spot is formed from which the measurements of the lines may be made.

The exposures may range from 20 seconds in the case of hydrogen lines to 30 minutes or more, 15 minutes being usually enough. As soon as it is complete, the above procedure is re-

[6] Grounded.

peated, and the plate moved into the second position. In this way, as many as six spectra can be taken on one plate, after which L is shut, I_2 warmed up, and air admitted to the camera. The cap P, which is on a ground joint, can now be removed, and the exposed plate seized and taken out with a special pair of forceps. A fresh plate is now immediately put in, P replaced, and the camera again exhausted, in which state it is left till the next operation.

Form of the Spectrum Lines

. . . The shape of the spot formed when undeflected rays from such a slit system strike a photograph surface normally is somewhat as indicated at a (Figure 7–4). When they strike the plate

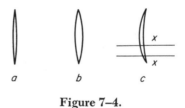

Figure 7–4.

obliquely, the image would be spread out in one direction, as in b. This would be the actual form in the apparatus, if the deflexions of the mean and extreme rays (i.e., the rays forming the centre and the tips) were identical. This is true of the magnetic field, since each cuts the same number of lines of force; but it is not so in the case of the electric deflexion. Since the form of the plates, and therefore roughly of the boundaries of the field, is rectangular, the extreme rays passing diagonally will be deflected more than the mean rays and the spot bent into the form shown at c. The convex side will be in the direction of the magnetic deflexion, as this is opposed to the deflexion causing the bend. The image on the plate will therefore be the part of this figure falling on the narrow slot in X–X; and as the apparatus is not exactly symmetrical, its shape in the spectra is the figure lying between the lines X–X in Figure 7–4, c.

Measurement of the Lines

The plates are measured against a standard Zeiss scale on a comparator designed by the late Dr. Keith Lucas and kindly lent by the Physiological Department. Some of the very faint lines, although easily visible to the unaided eye, were lost even with the lowest-power eyepieces obtainable. To measure these, an eyepiece giving a magnification of about $2\frac{1}{2}$ was designed by Dr. Hartridge, of King's College.

The general method of deducing mass from position has already been described.* Owing to some geometrical cause (probably analogous to a cause in optics), the more deflected edge of the line is always the brighter and sharper, and it is the distance of this from the register spot that is found to give the most reliable values. For the highest accuracy, owing to halation,[7] one must only compare lines of approximately equal intensity. As this edge is unfortunately not at right angles to the spectrum, measurements can never be regarded as absolute, unless extreme care is taken in the levelling of the spectrum on the comparator. So although theoretically it is sufficient to know the mass of one line to determine (with the correction curve) those of all others, in practice every effort is made to bracket any unknown line by reference lines and only to trust comparative measurements when the lines are fairly close together. Under these conditions, the accuracy claimed for the instrument is about one part in a thousand (see Figure 7–5).

* *Philosophical Magazine*, April, 1920, p. 453.
[7] Halolike reflections.

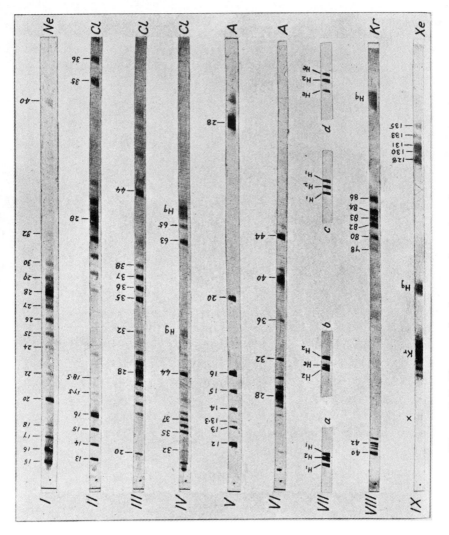

Figure 7–5. Photograph of traces from Aston's mass spectrometer.

Order of Results and Nomenclature

The various elements studied will be considered as far as possible in the order in which the experiments were performed. This order is of considerable importance, as in most cases it was impossible to eliminate any element used before the following one was introduced. Evacuation and washing have little effect, as the gases appear to get embedded in the surface of the discharge bulb and are only released very gradually by subsequent discharge.

The problem of nomenclature became serious when the very complex nature of the heavy elements was apparent. After several possible systems had been discussed, it was decided, for the present, to adopt the rather clumsy but definite and elastic one of using the chemical symbol of the mixed element with an index corresponding to its mass: e.g., Ne^{22}, Kr^{84}. This system is made reasonable by the fact that the masses of constituents of mixed elements have all so far proved whole numbers on the scale used.

In cases of particles carrying more than one charge, it will be convenient to borrow the nomenclature of optics and refer to the lines given by singly, doubly, and multiply charged particles, respectively, as lines of the first, second, and higher orders. Thus, the molecule of oxygen gives a first-order line at 32, and its atom first- and second-order lines at 16 and 8.

The empirical rule that molecules only give first-order lines *
is very useful in helping to differentiate between elementary atoms and compound molecules of the same mass. Some very recent results give indications that in certain exceptional cases it may break down, so that inferences made from it must not be taken as being absolutely conclusive.

* Joseph John Thomson, *Rays of Positive Electricity* (London: 1913), p. 54.

Oxygen (At. Wt. 16.00) and Carbon (At. Wt. 12.00)

On a mass spectrum, all measurements are relative, and so any known element could be taken as a standard. Oxygen is naturally selected. Its molecule, singly charged atom, and doubly charged atom give reference lines at 32, 16, and 8, respectively. The extremely exact integral relation between the atomic weights of oxygen and carbon is itself strong evidence that both are "pure" elements, and so far no evidence appears to have arisen to throw any doubt on this point. Direct comparison of the C line (12) and the CO line (28) with the above standards shows that the expected whole-number relation and additive law hold to the limit of accuracy, i.e., one part in a thousand; and this provides standards C^{++} (6), C (12), CO (28), and CO_2 (44). In a similar manner, hydrocarbons give the C_1 and C_2 groups already men-

TABLE 7–1. Table of Results

ELE-MENT	ATOMIC NUMBER	ATOMIC WEIGHT	MINIMUM NUMBER OF ISOTOPES	MASS OF ISOTOPES IN ORDER OF INTENSITY
H	1	1.008	1	1.008
He	2	3.09	1	4
C	6	12.00	1	12
N	7	14.01	1	14
O	8	16.00	1	16
Ne	10	20.20	2	20, 22, (21)
Cl	17	35.46	2	35, 37, (39)
A	18	39.9	(2)	40, (36)
Kr	36	82.92	6	84, 86, 82, 83, 80, 78
X	54	130.2	5	(128, 131, 130, 133, 135)
Hg	80	200.6	(5)	(197–200, 202, 204)

Note: Numbers in brackets provisional only.

tioned,* so that a fairly complete scale of reference is immediately available.

The Whole-Number Rule

The most important generalization yielded by these experiments is the remarkable fact that (with the exception of H_1, H_2, and H_3) all masses, atomic or molecular, element or compound, so far measured are whole numbers within the accuracy of experiment. It is naturally premature to state that this relation is true for all elements, but the number and variety of those already exhibiting it makes the probability of this extremely high.

On the other hand, it must not be supposed that this would imply that the whole-number rule holds with mathematical exactness, but only that the approximation is of a higher order than that exhibited by the ordinary chemical combining weights and is quite close enough to allow of a theory of atomic structure far simpler than those put forward in the past; for such theories were forced to attempt the explanation of fractions that now appear to be merely fortuitous statistical effects due to the relative quantities of the isotopic constituents.

Thus one may now suppose that an elementary atom of mass m may be changed to one of mass $m+1$ by the addition of a positive particle and an electron. If both enter the nucleus, an isotope results, for the nuclear charge is unaltered. If the positive particle only enters the nucleus, an element of next higher atomic number is formed. In cases where both forms of addition give a stable configuration, the two elements will be isobares.

The electromagnetic theory of mass asserts that mass is not generally additive but only becomes so when the charges are relatively distant from each other. This is certainly the case when the molecules H_2 and H_3 are formed from H_1, so that their masses will be two and three times the mass of H_1 with great exactness. (It must be remembered here that the masses given by these

* _Philosophical Magazine_, April, 1920, pp. 452, 453.

experiments are those of positively charged particles, H_1 being presumably a single particle of positive electricity itself, and that the mass of an electron on the scale used is .00054 and too small to affect the results.)

In the case of helium, the standard oxygen, and all other elements, this is no longer the case; for the nuclei of these are composed of particles and electrons packed exceedingly close together. The mass of these structures will not be exactly the sum of the masses of their constituents, but probably less, so that the unit of mass on the scale chosen will be less than that of a single hydrogen atom.

The Heavier Elements

The results hold out the probability of great complexity in elements of high atomic number, which has already been proved by entirely different methods in the case of lead. The present apparatus has a resolution factor too low to deal adequately with these; so attention is being given to elements within its scope and to which the analysis can be applied. Results are steadily accumulating, which will be published in due course.

In conclusion, the author wishes to express his indebtedness to the Government Grant Committee of the Royal Society for defraying the cost of some of the apparatus employed.

Summary

A positive-ray spectrograph capable of giving a focussed mass spectrum is fully described in detail and its technique explained.

The results of a provisional analysis of eleven chemical elements—H, He, C, N, O, Ne, Cl, A, Kr, X, Hg—are given, showing that of these the first five only are "pure," the others being apparently composed of various numbers of isotopic constituents, krypton containing no less than six.

With the exception of those due to H_1, H_2, and H_3, all masses measured, allowing for multiple charges, are exactly whole numbers within the error of experiment (O = 16).

The lines due to hydrogen indicate that the mass of the atom of this element is greater than unity on this scale and in good agreement with the chemical value 1.008. Reasons for this are suggested.

◆

8

TOWARD THE MODERN
VIEW OF MATTER

Aston's work has its place on the path by which scientists arrived at a new concept of matter within the boundaries of the atom. Chemists studied the reactions between different substances, while physicists measured the interactions between substances and radiations. Chemical reactions now appeared attributable to "superficial" effects, while the responses to physical radiations were interpreted as coming from various depths inside the molecules and atoms. Chemists, dealing with material substances, considered that even the atom, at the limit of subdivision, retained the nature of mass. Physicists, attuned to the radiant forms of energy, concluded that at the ultimate limit mass and energy become interchangeable.

The use of spectroscopic measurements in chemical analysis and for the discovery of new elements had been greatly stimulated, as we have seen, by the work of Kirchhoff and Bunsen in the middle of the nineteenth century. As the number of these measurements increased, the need for a theoretical explanation grew. Lecoq de Boisbaudran had tried to correlate the light emitted by the heated substances with vibrations in their molecules. Another man whom we have not yet mentioned, Johann Jakob Balmer (1825–1898), was a little less ambitious; he wanted only to find a rule by which the many lines in the spectrum of an element could be expressed in one mathematical formula. Such a formula was:

$$\lambda = f \frac{m^2}{m^2 - n^2},$$

where λ is the wave length of the spectral lines, m and n are low whole numbers, e.g., from 1 to 6, and f is a constant factor. The constant $f = 3645.6$ when the wave length is measured in the small and convenient units introduced by the Swedish physicist Anders Jonas Ångström and therefore called "angstrom unit," which is a hundred-millionth of a centimeter (10^{-8} cm.). For example, by this formula the red line in the hydrogen spectrum requires $m = 3$ when $n = 2$, the blue line $m = 5$ when $n = 2$. Thus, the multiplicity of spectral lines was ordered by series, just as the increasing number of elements was ordered into periods of a comprehensive system. Balmer was following a path parallel to that begun by Lothar Meyer and Mendeleev.

However, he did not reach, or even attempt to reach, the goal of a complete system connecting the nature of the elements with their spectra. That goal was approached only after new discoveries had been made in apparently unrelated fields and had been interpreted by far-reaching theories.

Substances send out light when they are heated in the flame of a Bunsen burner or, at still higher temperatures, by an electric spark. A relationship existed between the energy of the emitted light, its wave length, and the temperature. Theories led to one formulation for this relationship at low temperatures and long waves and another for high temperatures and short waves, but each of these mathematical formulations was limited to its own region and became paradoxical when applied to the other.

Max Planck (1858–1947) succeeded in combining the two formulations into one that covered the entire range. The basis for his success was the introduction of a new mathematical unit —one that represented a smallest parcel of energy. The smallest particle of matter, the atom, thus received a companion, a smallest part of action (energy multiplied by time), named a "quantum." A few years later, Einstein identified this smallest parcel of energy in light rays, where he dubbed it the "photon."

In Planck's formula, the quantum was mathematically defined as the product of energy and the frequency of the radiation. Frequency, designated by the Greek letter ν, here means the number of waves that go out from a source of energy (say a light bulb) in one second. For instance, in one second, light travels a distance c of very nearly 300,000 km., which is the same as 3×10^{10} cm.; this is light's velocity, c. Waves of the length λ, in covering this distance, recur ν times. Thus wave length times frequency gives the velocity of light ($\lambda \cdot \nu = c$). Accordingly, blue light of $\lambda = 4 \times 10^{-5}$ cm. has the frequency

$$\nu = 3 \times 10^{10}/4 \times 10^{-5} = \tfrac{3}{4} \times 10^{15} \text{ waves per second.}$$

The frequency of occurrence of the waves is a very high number, while the length of the wave is a tiny fraction of a centimeter.

Planck's energy-time factor, symbolized by the letter h, also is an extremely small unit. But since h is constant, the quantum increases with the frequency (ν) and is largest for the shortest waves, that is, those with the highest frequency. The radiation which Wilhelm Konrad Roentgen discovered in 1895 is composed of waves that are about one ten-thousandth the length of the waves of light. (It takes about 8 volts to excite light, but 80,000 volts to produce Roentgen rays.) Therefore, from the standpoint of quantum theory these rays appear like bullets of high energy. Their power to penetrate objects like aluminum foils gives a measure of their frequency, which was called "hardness" before their wave nature had been definitely established.

Charles G. Barkla (1877–1944) measured the reflection and the scattering of Roentgen rays on various substances. He designated the "hard" radiation by the letter K, which he selected so that adjacent letters of the alphabet would be available when harder or softer rays would be found. Up to now, K has remained the "hardest" shell. This K radiation was observed, in 1904, with elements of lower atomic weights up to silver; heavier atoms gave the softer L rays with the same source of rays from a Roentgen tube. Henry Gwyn-Jeffreys Moseley (1887–1915) continued such studies with the elements from calcium to copper. He recorded the radiations on photographic plates and saw a relationship to the position of the elements according to their atomic weights. For the square root Q of the K series of radiations, he found that

> Q increases by a constant amount as we pass from one element to the next, using the chemical order of the elements in the periodic system. Except in the case of cobalt and nickel, this is also the order of the atomic weights. . . . We can confidently predict that in the few cases in which the order of the atomic weights A clashes with the chemical order of the periodic system, the chemical properties are governed by N (the sequential atomic number), while A itself is probably a complicated function of N. The close similarity between the X-ray spectra of the different elements shows that these radiations originate inside the atom, and have no direct connection with the complicated light-spectra and chemical properties which are governed by the structure of its surface.

Moseley published this in 1913. At that time, the concept of the atom had changed from a bold hypothesis of indivisible units of matter to a well-founded theory of particles that could be measured and subdivided into smaller particles. Experimental results on the passage of electricity through gases at low pressure led J. J. Thomson to declare in 1899:

> I regard the atom as containing a large number of corpuscles. . . . In the normal atom, this assemblage of corpuscles forms a system which is electrically neutral. Though the individual corpuscles be-

have like negative ions, yet when they are assembled in a neutral atom the negative effect is balanced by something which causes the space through which the corpuscles are spread to act as if it had a charge of positive electricity equal in amount to the negative charges of the corpuscles.

The atom is here "regarded" as a composite unit in which negative corpuscles (that is, electrons) have their charge neutralized by "something" with a corresponding positive charge. This rather vague picture was made more definite by Ernest Rutherford (1871–1937) in 1912. From experiments with alpha particles originating in radioactive decay, he surmised that "it seems simplest to conclude that the atom contains a central charge distributed through a very small volume." In fact, a small positive central nucleus had already been suggested by Hantaro Nagaoka in 1904. This, together with Thomson's idea, now led Rutherford to consider the atom as analogous to a planetary system; the positive nucleus, as the sun, is surrounded by electrons which circle around the center like planets. Cloud-chamber experiments on the transference of electric charges to condensing droplets gave results that were consistently interpreted as measures of the charge and the apparent mass of electron and nucleus.

The "simplest" further assumption was that the electrons moved on circular paths around the nucleus. Niels Henrik David Bohr (1885–1962), the central figure of our present story, developed the model of the atom further to explain the origins of radiations.

Bohr developed the idea that electrons circle the nucleus on globular shells and that the jump of an electron from one such shell to the next adjacent one involves a change in energy that corresponds to the quantum of energy. By applying sufficiently concentrated heat energy, electrons near the outer shell could be lifted to the next higher level, and when they returned to a normal position, electromagnetic waves in the range of visible light were emitted. On the other hand, the very powerful Roentgen rays penetrated the outer shells and excited electrons of the *inner* shells. In atoms of high atomic weight, having heavy nuclei and many electron shells, the outer shells shield the inner K shell, which is why experimenters could not produce a K radiation from such atoms.

The formula $h\nu = W_1-W_2$ expresses radiation as caused by a quantum jump from energy level W_1 to W_2. Such jumps are always measured as whole numbers corresponding to the difference, in quantum units, between electron shells. The reason for the success of Balmer's formula, which associated whole numbers with the lines of the spectrum, now became obvious.

However, more spectral lines were discerned than could be explained from the original assumption of circular orbits. The next conceptual step, therefore, was to go from circles to ellipses;

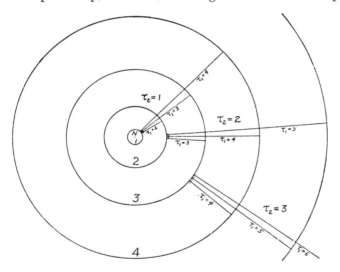

Figure 8–1. N represents the nucleus of the atom. The rings 1, 2, and 3 correspond to the orbits of the electron in the various steady states of motion. When an electron falls from one steady state to the next one of smaller radius of vibration, one quantum of energy is liberated. In the above spectral series, all the lines are formed by electrons falling from the second ring anl beyond, all the way to the first ring. The first line in the series is due to an electron falling from the second to the first ring; the second line, to an electron falling from the third to the first ring; and so on.

this was analogous to the reasoning of astronomers in explaining the orbits of the planets. In the formulas, as a consequence, an additional quantum number had to be introduced to account for the form of the ellipses; it was named the "azimuthal" quantum number, in allusion to the terms of astronomy.

Our Figure 8-1 shows a section through an atom with the nucleus surrounded by electrons on circular orbits; the arrows indicate the possibilities of quantum jumps between different levels. There is nothing either circular or elliptical in the observed spectral lines. It is the mathematical treatment of the measurements that is represented by the model, and the model makes it easier to understand the formulas and even to develop new ones. As experimental techniques continued to develop and disclosed new fine and hyperfine spectra, new quantum numbers and more complicated models became necessary—and possible.

◆

Roentgen Spectra and the Periodic System of the Elements [1]

NIELS BOHR AND D. COSTER

In a paper published in this journal,[*] one of the authors developed the principal aspects of a theory of atomic structure. On the basis of this theory, it seems possible to give an interpretation of optical as well as Roentgen spectra that is intimately related to an interpretation of the periodic system of the elements. Following the publication of this paper, the Roentgen-spectroscopic experimental material suitable for testing the theoretical concepts was considerably enriched through an investigation by the other author, and its relationship to theory was discussed in a recently published paper.[†] This brought to light several interesting re-

[1] *Zeitschrift für Physik*, Vol. 12 (1923), pp. 342–349.
[*] N. Bohr, *ibid.*, Vol. 9 (1922), p. 1.
[†] D. Coster, *Philosophical Magazine*, Vol. 43 (1922), p. 1070; Vol. 44 (1922), p. 546.

sults. In the present joint paper, the comparison of the experimental material with the theory is gone into somewhat more thoroughly than was the case in the studies cited, taking into consideration particularly the relevance of Roentgen spectra for the interpretation of the periodic system.

Theoretical Concepts of Atomic Structure

The theory is based on a classification of the electron orbits in the atom by means of comparison with the stationary states of an electron which executes a central motion. The orbits are designated by the symbol n_k. n represents the so-called "main quantum number," which, in the limiting case where the central motion becomes a simple periodic Kepler motion,* is the only factor determining the energy, as may be seen in the Balmer formula for the hydrogen spectrum. As is well known, the "azimuthal quantum number" k, whose effect on the energy depends on the deviation of the motion from a simple periodic one, defines the angular momentum of the electron about the center of the orbit. The introduction of this quantum number, of course, is the basis of Sommerfeld's theory of the fine structure of the hydrogen lines; this fine structure is due to the circumstance that, because of the relativity modification of the laws of mechanics, even the orbit of a single electron about a positive atomic nucleus is not strictly periodic, but can be described as a Kepler ellipse which executes a slow rotation in its plane. A survey of the number of electrons in the normal atom which, according to the theory, belong to the different types of n_k orbits, is given in Table 8–1. Concepts of atomic structure are expressed here which, apart from the characteristic new features, exhibit many similarities to the concepts that form the basis of the investigations on Roentgen spectra by Sommerfeld and Vegard.

It will be apparent that the electron orbits are arranged in groups that belong to the same value of the main quantum num-

* As in the sun's planets.

TABLE 8–1.

Δ^{n}_{k}	1_1	$2_1\,2_2$	$3_1\,3_2\,3_3$	$4_1\,4_2\,4_3\,4_4$	$5_1\,5_2\,5_3\,5_4$	$6_1\,6_2\,6_3\,6_4\,6_5\,6_6$	$7_1\,7_2$
1 H	1						
2 He	2						
3 Li	2	1					
4 Be	2	2					
5 B	2	2 (1)					
10 Ne	2	4 4					
11 Na	2	4 4	1				
12 Mg	2	4 4	2				
13 Al	2	4 4	2 1				
18 A	2	4 4	4 4				
19 K	2	4 4	4 4	1			
20 Ca	2	4 4	4 4	2			
21 Sc	2	4 4	4 4 1	(2)			
22 Ti	2	4 4	4 4 2	(2)			
29 Cu	2	4 4	6 6 6	1			
30 Zn	2	4 4	6 6 6	2			
31 Ga	2	4 4	6 6 6	2 1			
36 Kr	2	4 4	6 6 6	4 4			
37 Rb	2	4 4	6 6 6	4 4	1		
38 Sr	2	4 4	6 6 6	4 4	2		
39 Y	2	4 4	6 6 6	4 4 1	(2)		
40 Zr	2	4 4	6 6 6	4 4 2	(2)		
47 Ag	2	4 4	6 6 6	6 6 6	1		
48 Cd	2	4 4	6 6 6	6 6 6	2		
49 In	2	4 4	6 6 6	6 6 6	2 1		
54 X	2	4 4	6 6 6	6 6 6	4 4		
55 Cs	2	4 4	6 6 6	6 6 6	4 4	1	
56 Ba	2	4 4	6 6 6	6 6 6	4 4	2	
57 La	2	4 4	6 6 6	6 6 6	4 4 1	(2)	
58 Ce	2	4 4	6 6 6	6 6 6	4 4 1	(2)	
59 Pr	2	4 4	6 6 6	6 6 6 2	4 4 1	(2)	
71 Lu	2	4 4	6 6 6	8 8 8 8	4 4 1	(2)	
72 —	2	4 4	6 6 6	8 8 8 8	4 4 2	(2)	
79 Au	2	4 4	6 6 6	8 8 8 8	6 6 6	1	
80 Hg	2	4 4	6 6 6	8 8 8 8	6 6 6	2	
81 Tl	2	4 4	6 6 6	8 8 8 8	6 6 6	2 1	
86 Nt	2	4 4	6 6 6	8 8 8 8	6 6 6	4 4	
87 —	2	4 4	6 6 6	8 8 8 8	6 6 6	4 4	1
88 Ra	2	4 4	6 6 6	8 8 8 8	6 6 6	4 4	2
89 Ac	2	4 4	6 6 6	8 8 8 8	6 6 6	4 4 1	(2)
90 Th	2	4 4	6 6 6	8 8 8 8	6 6 6	4 4 2	(2)
118 Y	2	4 4	6 6 6	8 8 8 8	8 8 8 8	6 6 6	4 4

Note: By 1925 the even distribution of the electrons over the subgroups was abandoned on the basis of the Roentgen spectra; the new rule provided a stepwise increase by 4 electrons. Thus, element 86, now designated by Em = Emanation instead of Nt = Niton, was represented by the following electron arrangement:

2 | 2 6 | 2 6 10 | 2 6 10 14 | 2 6 10 | 2 6

The boldly projected element 118 would presumably be characterized as follows:

2 | 2 6 | 2 6 10 | 2 6 10 14 | 2 6 10 14 | 2 6 10 | 2 6

ber *n*. The formation of these groups, in going to elements of higher atomic number, is related to the regularities that occur in the periodic system. One essential feature in this is that the groups are in turn divided into subgroups, which correspond to the different values of the azimuthal quantum number *k*. The reason for the typical deviations from simple periodicity in the system of the elements (families of the iron and platinum metals as well as of the rare earths) is assumed to be (1) the gradual addition of new types of electron orbits with the same main quantum number as that of the groups of electron orbits already present in preceding elements, which causes (2) the progressive stepwise formation of these groups. A survey of the periodic system that exhibits these features especially clearly is given in Figure 8–2,* where the elements belonging to the same period of the system are arranged in vertical columns. Elements in successive columns that can be regarded as homologous in their chemical as well as their optical characteristics are connected by straight lines. Series of successive elements that assume a special position in that their inner groups are being built up are enclosed in square brackets.

The arrangement of Table 8–1 is based, in its main features, on considerations of a general nature which are explained in the paper mentioned above. In the working out of details, an intensive investigation of series spectra plays an essential part. In

* Cf. N. Bohr, *Three Essays on Spectra and Atomic Structure*, p. 132, Fig. 5, where a more detailed explanation of this figure can be found. Not taken into account either in the schematic representation or in the figure is the note by Dauvillier, C. R., May, 1922, mentioned in the supplement to these essays, on the observation of some weak lines in the Roentgen spectrum of an element of atomic number 72 in a mixture of rare earths, for this observation can hardly be regarded as definitely proved. The presence of an element between Lu (71), whose highest valence is 3, and Ta (73), whose highest valence is 5, with chemical properties similar to Lu, would represent a deviation from the otherwise general rule that the highest valence in the transition from one element to the following one never increases by more than one unit—a rule that has a direct explanation in the generally assumed concepts of atomic structure (cf. also C. R. Bury, *Journal of the American Chemical Society*, Vol. 43 [1921], p. 1902).

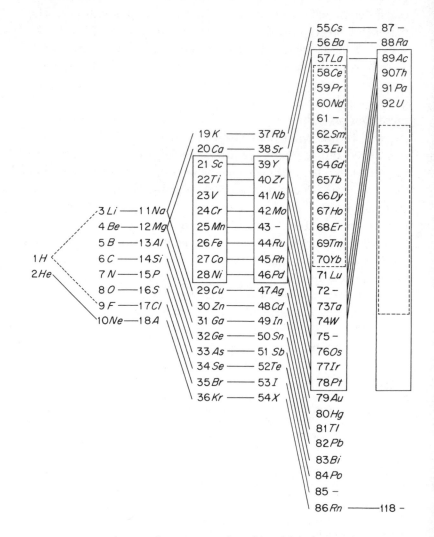

Figure 8–2. The new periodic table of the elements.

these spectra, again, although the gradual formation of inner electron groups is clearly reflected, the direct information that can be obtained from the series spectra concerns primarily the gradual addition of those electron orbits of new types by which the steps of the formation are introduced. Correspondingly, in Table 8–1, essentially only those elements are indicated that are the initial steps of the formation; besides, whenever the spectral material does not allow one to draw a unique conclusion regarding the number of electrons in the outermost groups, the numbers of electrons which correspond to the highest quantum orbits are shown in parentheses. The further formation of the groups is indicated only by its final result; but the description of the completely formed groups, also, still contains many uncertainties at this time, especially in regard to the finer interaction of electron motions within the same main group and its subgroups. Without entering into this question further here, we merely want to point out that the general assumptions on the nature of this interaction, introduced in the paper mentioned above and discussed there in more detail, provide a criterion, based on the correspondence principle, for a theoretical understanding of the typical laws that govern emission and absorption spectra in the Roentgen region, and whose main features were explained by Kossel's formal theory.

Classification of Roentgen Spectra

As explained in the paper by Coster cited above, it has been possible in the case of a large number of elements to obtain a classification of the Roentgen spectra based on the fact that the frequency v of each line can be represented as the difference between two spectral terms, T' and T''. In agreement with the principles of the quantum theory of line spectra, these spectral terms —multiplied by h—are interpreted as energy levels of an atom which, by the removal of an electron from an inner group, has been taken out of its normal state.

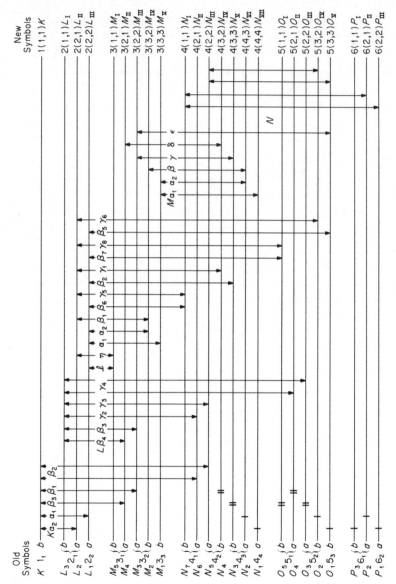

Figure 8–3.

Figure 8–3 gives a survey of the characteristic Roentgen spectrum to be expected for the inert gas radon (86). The spectral lines are indicated in the usual manner by vertical arrows, while the horizontal lines represent the levels. Only those lines are shown that were actually measured for several elements in the vicinity of this inert gas. At the same time, the figure gives a survey of the spectrum of the elements in the vicinity of the rare gases xenon and krypton. The levels that disappear in going to elements of lower atomic number between radon (86) and xenon (54) are shown in the figure by one vertical line, and the levels that disappear in addition between xenon (54) and krypton (36) are designated by two lines.

As indicated in the figure, the symbols used to designate the levels have been changed from those used in the preceding papers. First, the sublevels that belong to the same group of levels are designated by Roman numerals in the sequence in which they gradually occur with increasing atomic number in the Roentgen spectra of the elements. Further, each level has attached to it a numerical symbol of the form $n \, (k_1, k_2)$. Later, we shall discuss in more detail the relationship of these symbols to the theory of atomic structure. Here, we only want to point out that the levels that were used in Figure 8–3 for representing the spectra of each of the three inert gases are all characterized by those values of n and the k's that, in Table 8–1 above, occur as values of the quantum numbers n and k for the electron orbits in the atoms of these elements. We observe further that the occurrence of lines that correspond to combinations between the levels is governed by the rule that the number k_1 always changes by one unit in the transition process, while k_2 either changes by one or remains constant. These rules are equivalent to the rules that were expressed in Coster's earlier work by means of the old symbols, and formally they correspond precisely to the rules that were formulated in the same time by Wentzel. The numerical values introduced for k_1 and k_2 are equal to the values of the numbers n and m used by this author for the classification of the levels. However, we shall interpret their theoretical significance in a somewhat different way.

Determination of Energy Levels from the Experimental Material

The results of the presently available measurements of Roentgen spectra allow us to calculate the energy levels of a large number of elements with considerable precision. . . .

◆

Bohr and Coster then provide a table detailing the experimental investigations of other scientists upon which they based their calculations of the energy levels of various elements according to the methods discussed in their article.

PART II

AFFINITY
AND REACTIVITY

9

ABOUT CHEMICAL
CHANGE

So far, we have seen milestones along paths that led to the modern view of the structure of atoms and order among the elements. Now we are about to go back again in time and start upon another broad road in the history of chemistry: the road that led to our current views of chemical change. We shall be concerned with the development of concepts of chemical affinity, attraction, and reactivity. In short, now that we have glimpsed the stuff of which matter is formed, we are obliged to ask why it interacts chemically.

When the idea of elements was first clearly formulated, it signified the "real substance" in all things, or the unity in apparent diversity. Such, we remember, was the element of Thales (water) and of Anaximenes (air). Both ideas expressed the notion that change must be bound to something that remains essentially constant.

Heraclitus proclaimed that the principle of fire was much more suitable as a universal agent, because it accounted for change.

Empedocles took all three elements of antiquity—water, air, fire —and added earth as a fourth "root" for all matter. But was it enough to recognize the universal basis of matter? The philosophers had to consider what it was that united and separated the elements and caused reality to undergo change. With the forces of love and strife, Empedocles introduced a pair of active opposites, forces that could produce change. In a similar manner, ancient Chinese thinkers had represented a universal pair of opposites in the concepts of Yin and Yang. The Chinese diagram shown in Figure 9–1 combines symbols of these opposites with the five elements.

We have seen that the idea of opposite qualities, hot–cold and dry–wet, was also used for the elements themselves. Strangely enough, these opposites actually form a kind of bond between the elements, and still more strangely, the philosophers said nothing about the way in which the qualities could be supposed to be combined in each of the elements.

Love and strife, as human emotions, are hardly attributable to all of nature. So the mechanists replaced them by forces of attraction and repulsion. Attraction between chemical substances was called "affinity," which means kinship. Substances that were akin to each other were supposed to attract each other. However, eighteenth-century experiences with magnets and electricity seemed to show that attraction occurs between opposites. Newton once posited that particles of matter repel each other; Dalton felt elated about his discovery that only particles of the same kind do this, not particles of different kinds. Dalton could thus explain the physical behavior of gas mixtures; but he did not advance toward the problem of chemical attraction and repulsion, the underlying phenomena of chemical change on the organic and the inorganic levels.

In the latter part of the eighteenth century, the word "affinity" was little used; it was too reminiscent of those "hidden forces" that Newton had rejected so as to eliminate the mysterious from the scientific view of nature. Physicists and chemists sought to

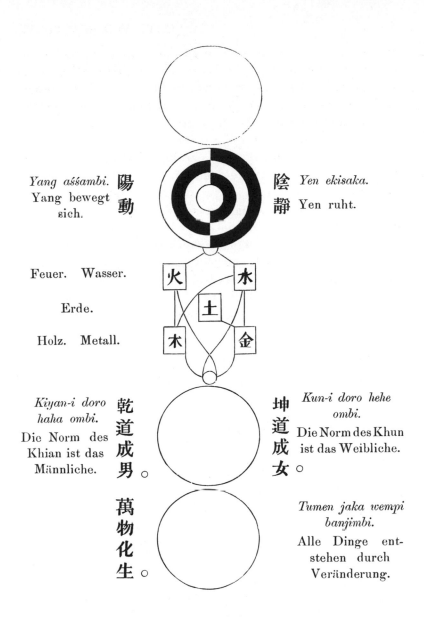

Yang *aśśambi.*
Yang bewegt sich.

陽動

陰靜

Yen ekisaka.
Yen ruht.

Feuer. Wasser.

Erde.

Holz. Metall.

Kiyan-i doro haha ombi.
Die Norm des Khian ist das Männliche.

乾道成男

萬物化生

坤道成女

Kun-i doro hehe ombi.
Die Norm des Khun ist das Weibliche.

Tumen jaka wempi banjimbi.
Alle Dinge entstehen durch Veränderung.

Figure 9–1.

remove the stigma of mystery from the concept of affinity by dividing it into categories. In his systematic presentation of all chemical knowledge, Antoine François Fourcroy (1801) formulated ten laws for attractions of various kinds. Other theorists designed tables in which they arranged acids and bases in the order of their "attractions."

Such tables had some value in showing relationships in chemical substances, and they were rightly called "Tables of Rapports." However, they were not so successful as the tables of the elements based on atomic weight, which we have discussed. While atomic weights are constant, relative affinities change, being subject to the influence of external conditions.

In 1803 Claude Louis Berthollet therefore suggested a different approach. Since outside factors had such an important influence on chemical reactions, affinity should not be considered something of an entirely separate kind. Instead, as Marcelin Berthelot summarized his predecessor's work,

> Berthollet tried to reduce the formations and decompositions of the substances to purely mechanical principles that are independent of any special notion of affinity. He endeavored to bring the influence of the conditions that are due to cohesion into the right light, for example, insolubility, crystallization, volatility.

In Berthollet's view, then, chemical interaction resulted from the action of mass and not from a special chemical "force." Since by this definition affinity does not exist, no one need ask whether it attracts similar or opposite substances.

But if this were true, how could one account for the seeming differences in the vigor of various reactions? Some combinations occurred with an appearance of being stronger than others; the reactions might even show vehemence: for example, the heat developed in combustion or the explosive reaction of hydrogen with oxygen. Were such signs of vigor not similar to those observed when opposite electricities combined to produce heat and sparks? In fact, chemical affinity could be considered an electric effect. And seen from this standpoint, Berthollet was right in trying to abolish the idea of affinity as something entirely different from other physical "forces"; he was wrong in the specific explanation, but not in his general aim.

Early in the nineteenth century, scientists knew that attractive and repulsive forces characterized so-called "electrified metal surfaces." When such surfaces were immersed in a salt liquefied by solution or fusion, the metallic bases of the salt were attracted by the negative surface, the oxygen and acidic part by the positive surface. In 1812 Humphry Davy concluded: "These attractive and repulsive forces are sufficiently energetic to destroy or suspend the usual operation of elective affinity."

In 1813 and 1814, Berzelius expressed his own views of an electrical basis for affinity in these words:

What we call chemical affinity, with all its changes, is nothing but the action of the electric polarity of the particles, and electricity is the first cause of all chemical activity. . . . Every chemical action is basically an electrical phenomenon, depending on the electric polarity of the particles.

He continued:

If these electrochemical views are correct, it follows that every chemical combination is wholly and solely depending on two opposing forces, positive and negative electricity, and every chemical compound must be composed of two parts combined by the agency of their electrochemical reaction, since there is no third force. Hence it follows that every compound body, whatever the number of its constituents, can be divided into two parts, one of which is positively and the other negatively electrical.
. . . In the present state of our knowledge, the most probable explanation of combustion and of the ignition resulting from it is that in every chemical combination there is a neutralisation of opposite electricities, and this neutralisation produces fire in the same way as it is produced in the discharges of the electric bottle [Leyden jar], the electric pile, and lightning, without being accompanied, in these latter phenomena, by chemical combination.

Berzelius arranged all the 53 then-known elements in a series from the most electronegative, oxygen, to the most positive, potassium. But there were many problems. For instance, oxygen and sulphur are both negative; yet they combine with each other with greater "force" than, for example, sulphur with the positive copper. Berzelius tried several modifications of the general theory, but later on he dismissed the whole thing as just a play of the imagination. He gave up because he did not find the way from the general assumption to a quantitative measurement of electrochemical polarity.

Michael Faraday broke ground in this direction through his concept and measurement of the *electrochemical* equivalent. Elements that were chemically equivalent were shown to carry the same amount of electricity. Moreover, Faraday discovered that he could reverse the process and measure electricity in chemical terms. The quantity of hydrogen and oxygen developed by electrolysis (of water made conductive by sulphuric acid) could be used as a measure of the "power" of electrical input. He called an apparatus for the chemical measurement of electricity a "voltameter." With the nomenclature developed later, it should be named a "coulometer," because Volta's name is used for the electrical potential, while Coulomb's name is associated with electrical current.

Faraday found that the chemical action of electrical current was directly proportional to "the absolute quantity of electricity which circulates." Furthermore, he saw that this sort of chemical change was indeed reversible: the decomposition of an electrolyte by applying electricity through metallic electrodes can be turned around, inasmuch as electrolytes generate electricity in the metallic conductors if the experiment is properly arranged.

Berzelius had started on his electrochemical theory by considering the heat of chemical reactions as the effect of electricity. Faraday seemed to proceed in the opposite direction, with the additional concept of equivalence in quantities; that is to say, a certain amount of heat, or work, resulted in a certain amount of electricity. In fact, the equivalence of heat and mechanical work had been a great topic in the late eighteenth and the early nineteenth centuries. Experiments in producing heat mechanically, by Benjamin Thompson (later named Count Rumford), in 1798, were soon amplified in calculations based on the steam engine, in which heat is converted into mechanical work. Sadi Carnot (1796–1832) proved that an ideal heat engine furnishes the same amount of work when heat descends from a higher to a lower temperature, regardless of whether steam or any other medium is used.

In the movement from mechanical work to heat and back again, a natural reversibility seemed disclosed. Was a similar reversibility not the sum and substance of chemical change? Lavoisier's theories, which explained chemical processes of respiration as combustion, stimulated Julius Robert Mayer (1814–1887) in 1842 to press the search for the equivalence of heat and work. With due consideration of Gay-Lussac's experiments on the expansion of gases, Mayer found that the fall of a weight from a height of 365 meters into a volume of water of equal weight would raise the water's temperature 1°C. The numerical value of this "mechanical equivalent of heat" was later revised from 365 to 426.85.

Actually, Mayer did not carry out any experiment; he brought known results together under a new form of an old concept: the principle of the conservation of energy. Carnot had arrived at the same concept, but in more limited form: "Always when motive power is destroyed, at the same time heat is produced in quantity exactly proportional to the quantity of motive power destroyed. Reciprocally, always when heat is destroyed, motive power is produced." So that the terms "destroyed" and "produced" should not be misunderstood, Carnot added that motive power is an invariable quantity in nature, changing its form but never being annihilated.

All these developments were related to the study of affinity. They have in common the quest for an understanding of reciprocity or reversibility in physical and chemical change. The process of conversion can proceed in one direction or in the opposite direction. Robert Boyle had already discovered the reversibility of a few chemical reactions. Joseph Black (1728–1799) extended this knowledge with his experiments on the "mild" and the "caustic" forms of lime and of magnesia. Conditions can be found in which mild calcium carbonate is decomposed into caustic lime and "fixed air"—i.e., carbon dioxide—while under other conditions lime unites with the gas and, becoming mild, reverts to the carbonate. Under intermediate conditions, the reaction goes partly one way, until it is limited by a counterreaction. An equilibrium is thus reached between decomposition and combination. Thus the equation can be read in either direction —as written, or from right to left:

$$\text{limestone} = \text{quicklime} + \text{fixed air}$$
$$\text{CaCO}_3 \qquad \text{CaO} \qquad \text{CO}_2$$

This concept of equilibrium was found to be generally applicable to chemical reactions. Where that equilibrium lies—i.e., how far it is from one or the other end of the complete directional reactions—can be understood as the effect of affinity.

From the standpoint of a "mechanical philosophy," Robert Boyle saw in matter and motion the ultimate "elements" and thus also the cause of affinity, reactivity, and change. Today, Boyle's candidates recur as matter and energy. The relationship between them becomes the guiding star of the ensuing chemical adventures. "What," each of the researchers may be imagined to ask, "are the general rules that apply to chemical change, regardless of the substances involved and valid for all?"

In the course of time, the answers to this question took affinity out of a connection with human feelings and converted it into a measurable force connected with other forces. The rules for this force were expressed in mathematical formulas. The individual character of specific substances became a constant factor with its specific response to the other forces. All this is said in somewhat antiquated language, speaking of "force" when actually energy is meant.

10

TOWARD A "CHEMISTRY WITHOUT SUBSTANCES"

We shall set out on this second broad path in the history of chemistry in the company of Pierre Eugène Marcelin Berthelot (1827–1907) and Léon Péan de Saint-Gilles (1832–1863), and for the first time in this book we shall become involved in organic chemistry. These men selected the reactions between an alcohol and an organic acid as representative examples of how affinity acts. They were not so much interested in the specific substances themselves as in discerning the various factors that influenced a reaction.

Berthollet had been particularly interested in reactions that involved a change in "cohesion"; that is, an alteration whereby a substance became insoluble or volatile and left the system as a precipitate or a gas. Berthelot, on the other hand, tried to answer the question: "What happens in a system that is homogeneous at the start and remains so during the whole reaction?" With this question in mind, he investigated the formation of what he called "ethers," the compounds formed between acids and alcohols (later named "esters").

In an ester, two carbon atoms are linked through an oxygen atom, and one of the carbon atoms carries another oxygen atom connected by a double bond. The term *ether* has been reserved for substances having a C — O — C group and no other double-bonded oxygen atom; for example:

AN ETHER

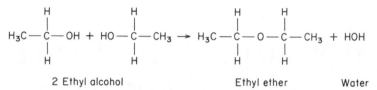

2 Ethyl alcohol   Ethyl ether   Water

AN ESTER

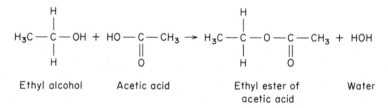

Ethyl alcohol   Acetic acid   Ethyl ester of   Water
                                        acetic acid

For at least a hundred years before the work of Berthelot and Saint-Gilles, it had been known that alcohol and acid can combine to form a new, "sweet" product, and Karl Wilhelm Scheele (1742–1786) had described some of its details in 1782, but nothing much had been done about its mode of formation since that time.

"Here," wrote Berthelot, "the reactions are slow, continuously progressing, and the products remain continuously with the ability to react with each other. The slowness of the reaction furthermore makes the products relatively stable, so that they can be isolated in the state in which they exist in the system." Therefore, he could measure the acid remaining in the slow ester-forming reaction by the fast salt-forming neutralization.

The first of the following selections cites some highlights

from Berthelot's extensive publications of 1862 and 1863. His general conclusion at the end of this work points the way to a physical chemistry and to Wilhelm Ostwald's ideal of "a chemistry without substances." The reports have been translated from the French.

◆

Researches on the Affinities of the Formation and Decomposition of Ethers [1]

M A R C E L I N   B E R T H E L O T
AND L É O N   P É A N   DE S A I N T - G I L L E S

Organic chemists have mainly endeavored to obtain new compounds to construct and to study reactions. All of us know how much our science has thereby been enriched through the cumulative labor of three generations of chemists.

Yet, while studying the compounds and the relationships of their formulas and their equivalents, the chemists neglected the general conditions of chemical mechanics which are basic for the formation and decomposition of the compounds, relying instead on the results of mineral chemistry.

However, the study of organic chemistry reveals unexpected facts—almost without any analogy in mineral chemistry—that are of greatest importance for the theory of affinity: the influence of time and the predominant role of certain conditions of equilibrium quite outside of those expressed by Berthollet's laws. These conditions and their effects are perhaps most impressive in the reactions of the ethers, especially their formations and their decompositions.

Ethers represent a new fundamental type that is as characteristic for organic chemistry as the salts are for inorganic. Ethers are formed by the combination of acids with alcohols, and these

[1] *Annales de Chimie* (3), Vol. 65 (1862), pp. 385–422; Vol. 66 (1862), pp. 5–110; Vol. 68 (1863), pp. 225–359.

can be regenerated by decomposition; the similarity with salts formed from bases and acids has often been mentioned. Besides, ethers, like salts, can show double decompositions, at least in some cases, with each other as with salts.

Closer examination shows, however, that the analogy between ethers and salts is only superficial. . . . Thus, a volatile alcohol in an ether is not immediately replaced by a solid base, whereas this occurs in a salt with a volatile basis; the volatile alcohol is only slowly and progressively replaced by the base. Also, insoluble or volatile salts that can be formed at the expense of ethers do not occur immediately. For example, calcium chloride does not directly precipitate an ether of oxalic acid; barium chloride does not immediately form precipitates with the ethyl ethers of sulphuric acid; ethyl chloride, although a gas at room temperature, does not form on contact of an alkali chloride with a solid ether, etc.

Nevertheless, the affinities for the direct combination of acids with alcohols are generally very weak. Ethers are so little stable that not only weak bases, but even water causes decomposition.

The fundamental difference between ethers and salts seems to us to be due to two causes: first, the absence of electrical conductivity of alcohols and ethers; and [secondly] the small heat of reaction between alcohol and acid.

The Existence of a Limit

When an alcohol is brought into contact with an acid, a combination occurs with varying velocities, depending on the physical conditions of the experiment. Acid and alcohol neutralize each other slowly and yield two new products, water and other compounds. As the reaction proceeds, it slows down and gradually approaches a definite limit. This limit does not coincide with a complete saturation of the acid by the alcohol.

When the water is removed, the reaction between acid and alcohol can proceed to the end, like the reaction between an acid and a base. In the presence of water, the formation of ether stops at a definite limit. This limit is almost independent of temperature and pressure so long as the system remains liquid.

Generally speaking, in a system formed of acid, alcohol, neutral ether, and water in any proportions, the limit of the reaction is governed almost completely by the relationship between the equivalents of these substances and is almost independent of their individual nature.

In the mixture of one equivalent of acid with several equivalents of the alcohol, the amount of ether at first grows with the number of alcohol equivalents, although only one equivalent can enter into the compound. Experiments show that in the presence of excess alcohol, the amount of acid not consumed for forming the compound is in inverse proportion to the total quantity of alcohol.

In the mixture of one equivalent of alcohol with several equivalents of acid, the amount of etherified alcohol grows with the quantity of acid . . . and in inverse proportion to the total quantity of the acid.

Let us now consider the role of water in etherification. When one equivalent each of alcohol and acid are mixed with water, ether is formed, but its quantity diminishes as the quantity of water is increased without becoming zero, however large the excess of water. The decrease is continuous, without jumps, in a progression that changes much more slowly than the equivalents of water added to the system. This shows clearly the influence of the chemical mass of the excess water above the equivalents necessary for the reaction.

We have shown that the quantities of ether formed or remaining in the most varied systems are independent of the individual nature of the constituent acids and alcohols. The ideas of particular individual affinities, usually considered so important in etherification, must therefore yield to a very simple, very general concept mainly based upon the equivalents.

◆

Two Norwegian scientists, the mathematician and physicist Cato Maximilian Guldberg (1836–1902) and the chemist Peter Waage (1833–1900), took the next step on the path to a chemistry without specific substances.

Like Berthelot and Saint-Gilles before them, they sought to know what factors, other than the chemical composition of reacting substances, influenced the reaction. They were stimulated to undertake their "studies on affinity" by the first publication of Berthelot and Saint-Gilles in 1862. Guldberg and Waage considered combinations between hypothetical substances; to wit: "When the same masses of the acting substances are present in different volumes, the effect of these masses is inversely proportional to these volumes." What they were saying, in other words, was that the effect is proportional to the *concentrations* of the acting substances. As a consequence, equilibrium is reached when the "force" driving the reaction in one way is equaled by that which drives it from the opposite direction.

Affinity, or chemical attraction, is only one among several factors that determine the outcome of a chemical reaction. Guldberg and Waage were mainly concerned with temperature and what they called "mass"—actually the concentration of the reactants.

The chemical reaction of any compound AB with any compound CD at any given temperature is determined by the resultant of all the attractive forces. The individual character of the substances then expresses itself in the numerical value of this "resultant," which Guldberg and Waage call the "coefficient of affinity" and designate by the letter K. After elaborating the general principle, they proceed to several series of experiments. But this way of going from theory to experiment must not be misunderstood as contrary to accepted scientific methods. In fact, the experiments of many previous investigators provided the basis for the theory. The authors refer especially to Heinrich Rose (1795–1864), the German chemist who discovered many special properties of the element he named "niobium." Another reference in the paper is to Henri Victor Regnault (1810–1878) and his work on reactions between steam and metals or their sulphides. Regnault is particularly famous for his researches on the physical properties of gases, between 1847 and 1870.

This paper has been rendered into English from a German translation of the original article.

◆

Researches on Chemical Affinities [2]

CATO M. GULDBERG AND PETER WAAGE

When A and B combine with each other by addition, the compound AB has to be considered as resulting from attractions. In the simple substitution according to the formula $AB + C = AC + B$, the formation of AC is produced mainly by the attractions between A and C; however, other attractions act between the other substances present, and the force that leads to the formation of AC is the resultant of all these attractions. At a given temperature, this force can be considered as constant, and we represent its magnitude by the letter K, which we call the coefficient of affinity of the reaction.

Similarly, in the double decomposition $AB + CD = AC + BD$, the force producing the new substances is the resultant of all the attractions between A, B, C, D, AB, BC, AC, BD, and the resulting force K is the coefficient of affinity.

In the reaction $A + B = A' + B'$, the force leading to A' and B' is proportional to the coefficient of affinity, but it also is a function of the masses A and B. From our experiments, we have concluded that the force is proportional to the product of the active masses of A and B. Designating these active masses of A and B by p and q, the force $= k \cdot p \cdot q$.

[2] *Ostwald's Klassiker der exakten Wissenschaften,* Nr. 104 (Leipzig, 1899). The first of the three papers was in Norwegian and dated 1864, the second in French, 1867, the third in German and Norwegian, dated 1879. The first two were translated into German by R. Abegg and edited together with the third one.

This force kpq, or the force between A and B, is not the only one effective during the reaction. Other forces tend to retard or accelerate the formation of A' and B'. Let us, however, assume the other forces do not exist, and let us see how the formulations will look in that case.

Suppose the active masses of A' and B' are p' and q' and the coefficient of affinity of the reaction $A' + B' = A + B$ is K'; then the force of the regeneration of A and $B = K'p'q'$.

The relationship between K and K' can be found by experimental measurement of the active masses p, q, p', q'. On the other hand, when the ratio K'/K has been formed, the result of the reaction can be precalculated for any initial state of the four substances.

Action of Insoluble Salts on the Soluble Ones

We have studied mainly the decomposition of barium sulphate and potassium carbonate and the formation of these two salts by the decomposition of barium carbonate with potassium sulphate.

By taking 100 molecules of barium sulphate and 100 molecules of potassium carbonate, a definite limit value is found; for example, 20 molecules of barium carbonate. Starting with 100 molecules of barium carbonate and 100 molecules of potassium sulphate, the end value under the same condition is x. It is then very probable that the two end values correspond with each other, so that x ought to be $80 = 100 - 20$. The experiments do not give exactly this value; x is always found to be smaller than 80; however, this is due to special experimental difficulties. . . .

Regarding the influence of the masses, we find that the decomposition of barium sulphate is accelerated by increasing the potassium carbonate. Increasing the barium sulphate leads to an analogous result; however, the absolute increase of the end value is much smaller. A complete decomposition of barium sulphate can be achieved by a sufficiently large excess of potassium carbonate, as Heinrich Rose has already observed (1855). Rose also found that the presence of much potassium sulphate completely prevents the action of potassium carbonate upon barium sulphate.

Research in this field is certainly more difficult and time-consuming and less productive than the discovery of new compounds, with which most chemists are now occupied. Nevertheless, in our opinion there is nothing that will bring chemistry more quickly to the rank of a really exact science than the research that is the subject of our work. All our wishes would be fulfilled if we succeeded through this work in directing the attention of chemists to a branch of chemistry that has been too much neglected since the beginning of this century.

◆

11

SYSTEM, ENERGY, AND ENTROPY

Sometimes the course of science may weave back and forth between highly general laws and minutely specific details. At a time when chemistry had just been clearly established as a separate system of facts, Berthollet endeavored to bring affinity back into community with all other forces. After the success of isolating pure substances, Berthelot in France and Guldberg and Waage in Norway searched for rules under which all substances could be united.

Two general laws of nature had been recognized by philosophers of ancient times, but the two seemed in conflict. The first law was that of conservation: specifically the conservation of the quantity of matter and the equality between cause and effect. The second law expressed the general tendency of things to run down—of springs to lose tension, of hot bodies to cool. Did these losses not contradict conservation? A detailed study of the circumstances showed there was no contradiction if one took the entire context into account, allowing for transformations and for exchanges with the environment. The conservation laws would hold true so long as one considered a system isolated from outside influences or any system in which all the influences operating were known.

In 1824, Sadi Carnot, of France, published his thoughts about the motive power of heat, or "fire," as he called it. The basis of his thinking was the demonstrated impossibility of a perpetual-motion machine. He wrote about "the impossibility of an indefinite creation of motive power without consumption of caloric [heat] or of any other agent whatsoever." From this, Carnot concluded concerning the action of heat that "the maximum motive power resulting from the use of steam is also the maximum motive power that can be obtained by any other means." This step—from steam to "any other means" with regard to motive power—was followed about forty years later by a similar generalization concerning a maximum evolution of heat in spontaneous chemical reactions.

In 1842, Julius Robert Mayer formulated his idea that "mechanical force" must have a fixed relationship to the heat it can create. In 1852, William Thomson (later Lord Kelvin) wrote "On a universal tendency in nature to the dissipation of mechanical energy." The year before, he had stated the principle that it was impossible to derive work from the heat of a body if that body was cooled "below the temperature of the coldest of the surrounding objects." Now he extended this principle to cosmic dimensions, besides applying it to common experiences. In friction, he said, "there is dissipation of mechanical energy, and full restoration to its primitive condition is impossible."

Through these theories ran the principle that certain kinds of change within systems were irreversible. Once a body has been cooled below the temperature of its environment, its remaining heat cannot be converted into mechanical work in that environment. There are limits upon action. These ideas became the pillars of a new field of science that Thomson called "thermodynamics." Rudolf Julius Emanuel Clausius (1822–1888) treated the subject under the title, "The mechanical theory of heat." Either heading indicates that the general topic is the interchange between heat and other forms of energy.

In the language of thermodynamics, a system is defined as "any finite body or collection of bodies, or any region, possessing energy, every part of which has a definite temperature." In thought and experiment we construct isolated systems; they are surrounded by perfectly closed envelopes. The isolated system, which does not interchange matter or energy with the outside, is one of the idealizations of thermodynamics; the other is reversible processes. With these scientific constructions, we can arrive at an understanding of actual, irreversible processes as a "universal tendency of nature."

In Clausius' mathematical treatment, the processes are considered in their smallest steps according to the rules of calculus. The smallest differential of heat, dQ, is something like the atom or quantum of heat; Clausius occasionally calls it a "heat element." He develops a new expression for something corresponding to Thomson's "universal tendency" by forming the quotient of dQ and the temperature at which dQ is absorbed. For this he uses the temperature T measured from absolute zero, which he accepts from the work of Regnault and others to be at $-273°$C.

In 1843, at the conclusion of experiments with electrical batteries and "the magneto-electrical effect," James Prescott Joule had written, "I shall lose no time in repeating and extending these experiments, being satisfied that the grand agents of nature are, by the Creator's fiat, indestructible; and wherever mechanical force is expended, an exact equivalent of heat is always obtained."

Yet in 1849 William Thomson still pondered the paradox of heat generated by friction, in view of "the opinion commonly held that heat cannot be *generated*, but only produced from a source where it has previously existed." Clausius, we shall see, clarified this situation by distinguishing between the "free heat" and the "heat consumed for inner work." To Carnot's deduction that heat passing to a body at lower temperature furnishes work,

Clausius added the law: Heat cannot be transferred from a body to a hotter body without the expenditure of work. This was essentially what he called the "second law of mechanical heat theory," the first law being that of Robert Mayer and others relating to the conservation of energy. For Clausius, these laws were so fundamental that he extended them from the isolated systems of the laboratory to the entire universe.

The essay that follows is translated from the German. At the outset, Clausius is concerned with establishing general formulas that describe change in a system in terms of heat and work.

◆

Concerning Several Conveniently Applicable Forms for the Main Equations of the Mechanical Heat Theory [1]

RUDOLF CLAUSIUS

1. The whole mechanical heat theory rests on two main theses: the equivalence of heat and work, and the equivalence of the transformations.

For an analytical expression of the first thesis, we think of any kind of body that changes its state, and we consider the quantity of heat that has to be imparted to it to effect the change of state. Designating this quantity of heat by Q, and counting heat given off from the body as negative absorbed heat, the element dQ of heat absorbed during an infinitely small change of state follows the equation:

$$dQ = dU + A\,dW$$

Here U means the entity which I first introduced into heat theory in my paper of 1850 and which I there defined as the sum of the added free heat and the heat consumed for inner work. W means the external work done during a change of state, and A the heat

[1] *Annalen der Physik und der Chemie*, Vol. 125 (1865), pp. 353–400.

equivalent for the unit of work; i.e., the caloric equivalent of work. Thus, AW is the external work measured in heat units or, according to my recently proposed more convenient nomenclature, the external work.

By designating this external work, for the sake of brevity, by a single letter,

$$AW = w,$$

the equation above can be written:

$$dQ = dU + dw. \tag{1}$$

For the simplest analytical expression of the second law,[2] we assume the changes undergone by the body as forming a cyclic process through which the body finally returns to its initial state. Again, dQ means an element of heat absorbed, and T the temperature, counted from the absolute zero, of the body at the moment when it absorbs this heat element, or, in case the body had different temperatures in different parts, the temperature of that part which absorbs dQ. When the heat element is divided by the corresponding absolute temperature and the differential thus obtained is integrated for the entire cycle, then this integral is represented by

$$\frac{dQ}{T} \geqq O, \tag{2}$$

where the equal sign is valid for those cases in which all changes in the cyclic process occur in a reversible manner, while for the cases of nonreversible changes the "greater" sign is valid.

2. The external work (w) done while the body goes from one given initial state to another state depends not only on the state at the start and at the end but also on the kind of transition.

The energy U of the body . . . behaves in an entirely different

[2] He means the second thesis above, the equivalence of transformations.

manner. When the states at the start and at the end are given, the change of energy is completely defined; it is not necessary to know how the change from one state to the other has occurred, since neither the pathway of the change nor whether it is reversible or irreversible has any influence on the change of energy.

If, according to equation 2, the integral dQ/T always becomes zero when the body returns reversibly from any initial state through any intermediates into the initial state, then dQ/T must be the complete differential of a quantity that depends only on the momentary state and not on the way by which the body came to it. By designating this quantity as S, we can write $dS = dQ/T$, or, integrating this equation for any reversible process through which the body can reach its present state, starting from the selected initial state and designating by S_o the value of S in the initial state,

$$S = S_o + \int \frac{dQ}{T}.$$

In searching for a significant name for S, we could say, similar to what we said of U being the heat and work content of the body, that S should be the transformation content of the body. However, I believe it is better to take the names of such scientifically important units from the classical languages so that they can be used unchanged in all modern languages; therefore I propose to designate S by the Greek word ἡ τροπή = the transformation, the entropy of the body.

I reserve for later on the special application of mechanical heat theory, and particularly of the law of the equivalence of transformations, to radiant heat.

In the meantime, I shall limit myself to mentioning one result: Imagine the same quantity that, relative to one body, I have called its entropy, consequently, with due regard to all circumstances, applied to the entire universe, and also that other, simpler concept, energy, applied at the same time: then the fundamental

laws of the universe that correspond to the two laws of mechanical heat theory can be pronounced in the following form:
1. The energy of the universe is constant.
2. The entropy of the universe strives toward a maximum.

◆

These two sentences combine the two general laws and proclaim them as valid for the largest system we can conceive, the universe. The law of conservation does not imply stagnation because of the law—that entropy is striving toward a maximum, but if ever that maximum were reached, it would mean the end. Clausius coined the word *entropy* for "the transformation content" with the meaning: the tendency to transformation gradually uses up this reservoir of "content" so that it accumulates where it can no longer cause transformations.

The dissipation of heat was the outstanding example of increasing entropy, but not the only phenomenon to which the law applied. Ludwig Boltzmann generalized the law further by stating that a disordered state of arrangements has a greater probability than regular order. Max Planck later followed Albert Einstein in the bold assumption that entropy is proportional to the logarithm of the calculated probability, and he wrote:

$$S = k \times \log W,$$

where W is the initial of the German word for probability and S is the entropy connected with the logarithm of W by the constant k.

In 1876, Josiah Willard Gibbs (1839–1903) based his study of "the equilibrium of heterogeneous substances" on the concept of entropy as developed by Clausius. All processes in nature go in the direction of an increase in entropy, which is measured by the loss of energy transformable into work divided by the lowest available temperature T. However, the quotation did not mean that Gibbs intended to pursue the extension of this concept to the whole universe; instead, he was concerned with applying it to "substances" and, in this selected portion of his studies on thermodynamics, to assemblies of substances in several phases: gases, liquids, and solids.

Such "heterogeneous substances," or inhomogeneous systems, had been the subject of Berthollet's work of 1803. Berthollet had pointed out that the formation of an insoluble or a volatile product determines the equilibrium reached in a chemical reaction. For any "isolated system," Gibbs developed two simple and interrelated rules using the concepts of energy and entropy.

These rules govern change in any system of substances. Gibbs mentioned specific chemicals only for the sake of example and in order to show the application of the general principle. Yet he did bring chemical specificity into the picture in the form of the "chemical potential."

The general concept of potential has had a long history in philosophy and physics. In electrochemistry, potential was exactly defined as the intensity factor, or voltage, which, when multiplied by the quantity of current, or amperage, gave the measure of electrical action. By way of comparison, the height of a waterfall would be the potential; the amount of water flowing over it, the amperage. The chemical potential of a pure substance was defined as the available energy per unit of mass. With the symbols that Gibbs uses, ϵ denotes energy and m denotes the mass of a substance S. The potential of a substance, then, is given by the smallest, differential change $d\epsilon$ of energy produced by the differential change dm of its mass, or with the symbol μ for the potential, $\mu = d\epsilon/dm$. These calculations and the discussion of chemical potential have been abridged from the article to favor the discussion of entropy.

◆

Thermodynamic Researches [3]

J. WILLARD GIBBS

V. On the Equilibrium of Heterogeneous Substances

Die Energie der Welt ist constant.
Die Entropie der Welt strebt einem Maximum zu.
—CLAUSIUS

The comprehension of the laws that govern any material system
is greatly facilitated by considering the energy and entropy of
the system in the various states of which it is capable. . . . The
difference of the value of the energy for any two states represents
the combined amount of work and heat received or yielded by the
system when it is brought from one state to the other. . . . The
difference of entropy is the limit of all the possible values of the
integral

$$\int \frac{dQ}{t},$$

(dQ denoting the element of the heat received from external
sources, and t the temperature of the part of the system receiving
it). . . . [These] varying values of the energy and entropy
characterize in all that is essential the effects producible by the
system in passing from one state to another. For by mechanical
and thermodynamic contrivances, supposed theoretically perfect,
any supply of work and heat may be transformed into any other
which does not differ from it either in the amount of work and
heat taken together or in the value of the integral

[3] Abridged from *Transactions of the Connecticut Academy of Arts and
Sciences*, Vol. 3 (1876–1878).

$$\int \frac{dQ}{t}.$$

But it is not only in respect to the external relations of a system that its energy and entropy are of predominant importance. . . . In the case of . . . mechanical systems . . . that are capable of only one kind of action upon external systems, viz., the performance of mechanical work, the function that expresses [this] capability . . . for . . . action also plays the leading part in the theory of equilibrium, the condition of equilibrium being that the variation of this function shall vanish. . . . So in a thermodynamic system (such as all material systems actually are), which is capable of two different kinds of action upon external systems, the two functions that express the twofold capabilities of the system afford an almost equally simple criterion of equilibrium.

Criteria of Equilibrium and Stability

The criterion of equilibrium for a material system that is isolated from all external influences may be expressed in either of the following entirely equivalent forms:

I. *For the equilibrium of any isolated system it is necessary and sufficient that in all possible variations of the state of the system which do not alter its energy, the variation of its entropy shall either vanish or be negative.*

II. *For the equilibrium of any isolated system it is necessary and sufficient that in all possible variations in the state of the system which do not alter its entropy, the variation of its energy shall either vanish or be positive.*

◆

The "criterion," translated into somewhat more popular form, states that an equilibrium is maintained when any change would require a special effort, but a careful reading of the form in which Gibbs expresses this will show how much more beautiful his statement is. Because it employs well-defined terms instead of general assertions, it has much greater meaning.

12

AFFINITY AND
THE NEW CHEMISTRY

In the thoughts of the earliest philosophers, chemical reactions were the expressions of invisible forces that resided in substances. These forces were specific, such as fire or strife. Although universal, they were native to substances and unique.

In the last decades of the nineteenth century, through the study of equilibriums and other properties of systems, considerable insight was gained into this old mystery of chemical affinity. It became clear that many factors figured in chemical reactions; a precise definition of chemical attraction was not so easily obtained.

The work of two men was particularly important to the continued growth of a "chemistry without substances"; they are Jacobus Henricus van't Hoff, a Dutch chemist who lived from 1852 until 1911, and Henry Le Châtelier, van't Hoff's French contemporary, who lived until 1936. Although we present a scientific paper by Le Châtelier only, van't Hoff was equally prominent in the general march along this historic path.

Early investigators regarded matter in motion as being the sole province of physics. For the most part, chemists were little influenced by this work in their search for systematic co-ordination in the field of "purely" chemical reactions. In this field, substances react with substances, and the "natures" of these substances have full play. They are influenced by physical conditions; Berthollet had tried to explain the results of affinity, or chemical attraction, as governed by the physical attributes of elasticity and solubility. Heat was later added as a decisive factor, and the development of thermodynamics led to the concept of entropy. All spontaneous events were now endowed with the tendency to increase the entropy at the expense, and out of the supposed reservoir, of free energy.

It was a significant indication of the new approach to dynamics and kinetics of chemical reactions when van't Hoff replaced the $=$ sign in a chemical equation by arrows pointing in both directions $\rightleftharpoons$. Physicists had long considered the solidity of matter to be a function of the constant and rapid movement of its particles. With the new sign, chemists expressed the movements of the substances participating in an equilibrium. And as a further parallel, when physicists obtained new insights into the structure of matter by investigating gases under extremely low pressure, chemists like van't Hoff derived general laws of solutions by considering the limit of the lowest concentrations. But for what other reasons was van't Hoff led to investigate the role of the *concentration* of the partners in a chemical reaction?

At first thought, it would seem plausible that a great affinity manifests itself in a high speed of reaction. Measuring the speed of a reaction would thus afford the means for determining the affinity involved. This thought was pursued by chemists for some time, but it proved misleading.

Ludwig Wilhelmy used a different approach. He was familiar with Newton's law of cooling and the form in which Johann Heinrich Lambert had expressed it in his book *Pyrometry*, published posthumously in 1788: the rate at which a hot body cools (that is, the descent of its temperature in time) is proportional to the difference in temperature between the body and its surroundings. Since the change is continuous, it must be formulated by a differential equation:

$$du = -a \, u \, dt,$$

where u stands for the temperature difference, dt the infinitesimal change in the time element t, and a the factor of proportionality.

Wilhelmy tried to establish the same form of relationship between a rate of change and the quantity of that which changes; he did this only for the one reaction he studied, the inversion (hydrolysis) of the common kind of sugar, saccharose.

Wilhelmy's work of 1850 was neglected until Wilhelm Ostwald drew attention to it some forty years later. In fact, Jacobus Henricus van't Hoff did not know of it in 1884 when he developed his own ideas about the laws governing the speed of chemical reactions. Intuitively, he arrived at a formula of the same form as Wilhelmy's. The difference, however, was that van't Hoff made his law quite independent of sugar or any other specific substance. The symbol C in his formula means the concentration of the reacting substance, whatever it may be.

Equally general was his law for the change of the equilibrium constant as the result of changes in temperature.

Van't Hoff showed that in its speed a chemical action proceeds proportionally to the "active masses," which in most cases are simply the concentrations of the partners involved. The factor of proportionality is determined by the affinity. Therefore, a fundamental relationship exists between the equilibrium constant, which is the ratio of the proportionality factors, and the energy factors, which reflect concentration of the partners. For van't Hoff, the relationship followed directly from the laws of thermodynamics.

Le Châtelier's work, coming at the time of van't Hoff's studies of the lower limits of concentration, was aimed at isolating the effects of additional factors on equilibrium. All these efforts had the same goal: the use of physical measurements and concepts to arrive at the meaning and effect of chemical affinity. If one likes, one can imagine these new researchers still asking themselves the old questions, "What is the secret of affinity? Why are some chemical substances attracted to each other, while others are not? How strong is that attraction? How is it influenced by other energies?"

Le Châtelier was aware of the work of many others who had sought answers to these elusive questions.

For instance, it had been shown that the influence of heat on chemical affinity can be made so great that it drives compounds apart into their components. In 1857, Henri Étienne Sainte-Claire Deville called it "the repulsive force of heat" and its effect "the dissociation of compound bodies." Thus, water is dissociated, or decomposed, in contact with silver heated to its melting point, as Regnault had stated. Sainte-Claire Deville found "that hydrated potash is entirely dissociated in passing across incandescent iron; that in the lower part there is really potassium, hydrogen, and oxygen."

Le Châtelier concluded from these and subsequent experiments that there is a general law of reaction to an action on a substance or system of substances. In simplified language, the law states that the substances change in a direction that is opposite to the action to which they are exposed. Thus, a mixture of nitrogen and hydrogen, put under pressure, will change in the direction of forming ammonia, because the volume is thereby reduced. This can be seen in the formula:

$$1N_2 + 3H_2 \rightarrow 2NH_3.$$

In this case, Le Châtelier's prediction—the "Principle of Le Châtelier"—actually served as a guide in the efforts to synthesize ammonia from the elements, started by Fritz Haber and Walther Nernst in 1904.

Le Châtelier's studies of chemical equilibrium are reported in the following passages, which have been translated from the French.

◆

Experimental and Theoretical Studies on Chemical Equilibrium [1]

HENRI LE CHÂTELIER

Henri Sainte-Claire Deville (*Leçons sur la dissociation*, 1864) was the first to recognize the universal importance of . . . the phenomena of equilibrium. All substances—even the most stable, like water or carbon dioxide—are subject to a limited decomposition at certain temperatures and pressures, or a "dissociation," to use the new word he introduced for a completely new idea in science. Not only did he indicate the existence of these phenomena; he also set forth the principles that should guide us to arrive at the governing laws. He pointed out the analogy [between association and] the physical phenomena of vaporization, fusion . . . and thus was able to foresee the existence of definite tensions of dissociation, analogous to the definite tensions of vaporization.

In this work, I have taken as my guide the idea that had led Sainte-Claire Deville to the discovery of the phenomena of dissociation, and I have sought to generalize it still more.

The Nature of Equilibrium; Reversibility

The chemical reactions, including changes of state, are also connected with phenomena of equilibrium. They can stop, before being complete, in a stable state that is independent of the prior states of the system; and the deformations of the system in equi-

[1] *Annales des Mines* (2), Vol. 13 (1888), pp. 157–382.

librium are reversible, i.e., the state of the system becomes the same again with the exterior conditions of the medium in which it is placed. . . .

The Factors of Equilibrium

The factors of chemical equilibrium are the same for all reactions and much less numerous than is often thought. They can be divided into two distinct categories:

1. The external factors of equilibrium, which can be changed in magnitude independently of the system that is in equilibrium. I shall show that there are three such factors—temperature, electromotive force, pressure—corresponding to the three forms of free energy: heat, electricity, and work.

2. The internal factors of equilibrium, which are intimately connected in their magnitude with the state of the system in equilibrium. They can be divided into three groups, according to whether they depend on the chemical nature, the physical state, or the condensation of the substances present; these are circumstances related to the internal energy of the substances. . . .

The Law of Opposition of Reaction to Action

After having established that any alteration of one of the three factors of equilibrium necessarily leads to a change of a system that was in equilibrium, the first question that arises is whether there is a correlation between the direction of the change of the system and the direction in which the factor varies. This correlation is very simple:

When one of the factors of equilibrium changes, any system that was in equilibrium undergoes a transformation in such a direction that, if it occurred by itself, it would change this factor in the contrary direction.

This is a purely experimental law; however, it is based on so many facts that it can be considered as very strong.

This law brings the reversible chemical phenomena into the class of reciprocal phenomena of Lippmann: a change of one of the factors leads to a deformation of the system and, reciprocally, a deformation of the system leads to a change of the factors.

I am going to describe this law by reviewing the several factors of equilibrium.

Temperature: Every increase in temperature imposes on a chemical system in equilibrium a transformation corresponding to an absorption of heat; i.e., a transformation that would produce a lowering of the temperature if it occurred by itself. This law has been given by van't Hoff for the chemical phenomena alone; I have shown that it is more general than its author thought.

Electricity: Every change of electromotive force exerted at one point of a system in equilibrium produces a change of the system, which, if it occurred by itself, would lead to a variation of the electromotive force in the contrary direction.

Example: The Peltier effect in a heterogeneous conductor; this is reciprocal to the phenomenon of thermoelectricity. Electrolysis: the imposed chemical decomposition tends to regenerate a current of opposite sign; this is the principle of secondary chemical batteries or accumulators. . . .

Pressure: The increase of pressure on any chemical system in equilibrium leads to a transformation that tends to reduce the pressure.

It is known that compression lowers or raises the melting point, depending on whether the melting is accompanied by an increase or a diminution of the volume.

The same is true for gaseous systems, whether homogeneous or not; compression leads to the condensation of vapors, to the combination of carbon dioxide with chalk, etc.

Condensation: The change in condensation of one of the elements causes a transformation in such direction that a certain quantity of that element disappears, so that its condensation can be diminished.

This is the mass action that is applicable so widely in chemistry.

The experiments by Berthelot on esterification and by Lemoine on the dissociation of hydrogen iodide have clearly shown that the addition of a new quantity of one of the substances already present in an equilibrized mixture increases the extent of that reaction which tends to consume the added substance.

This general law about the opposition of action and reaction . . . is only a generalization of the condition for the stability of equilibrium in mechanical systems.

◆

Thus, the generalization went from one influence to all that can be exerted on a system, and the system was extended from the chemical to the mechanical. Taking all this together, we see here the fruitful application of the concept expressed in the law of entropy.

13

AFFINITY, THE ATOM, AND THE MOLECULE

The early studies concerning the chemical meaning of affinity led to the conclusion that substances were in some way carriers of energy. One of the ways of explaining this was the "opinion" cited by William Thomson that heat resides in the substances. Dalton's pictures showed the atom surrounded by a heat sphere.

These ideas underwent a thorough change at the turn of the century. The new experiences on the passage of electricity through gases led to the concept of electrons. The atom was soon to appear as a heavy nucleus surrounded by electrons moving at high speed in prescribed orbits, as we remember from the discussion of Bohr's work at the close of Part I. The valence bonds that hold the atoms together in the compounds were now interpreted as being electronic. Joseph John Thomson, who still preferred to use the word *corpuscle* instead of *electron,* wrote in his book on *The Corpuscular Theory of Matter:*

> We see that on these views the valency of an element is not a constant quantity: it depends on whether the element is the electro-

positive or electronegative constituent of the compound, and even when the sign of the charge is the same, on the nature of the element with which it is in combination, an element having a smaller valency when combined with one of similar properties than when in combination with one from which it differs widely.

In the cases of chemical combination we have considered, we have supposed that there is a transference of corpuscles from one atom to the other and that the attraction between the positive and the negative electrification resulting from this transference helps to bind together the elements in the compounds.[1]

Chemists had regarded the bond between the atoms, indicated by a straight line, as being without direction. But now Thomson wrote:

On the electrical theory, however, the tubes of electric forces are regarded as having direction starting from the positive and ending in the negative atom; thus, if the hydrogen atoms are positively electrified in marsh gas and the chlorine atoms negatively electrified in carbon tetrachloride, the graphical formulas representing them would be

respectively, indicating that the carbon atom is not in the same condition in the two compounds, as in one case it is the terminus, in the other the origin of the tubes of electric force.

Gilbert N. Lewis (1875–1946) was most prominent among those who developed this approach to the problem of valency. Lewis worked out the kinships of properties and the chemical behavior of some of the simpler elements on the basis of their electron-shell structure. An atom with an unsatisfied outer shell

[1] Joseph John Thomson, *The Corpuscular Theory of Matter* (London, 1907), p. 127.

tends to enter into combination with other atoms to complete its outer shell. There was evidence, to begin with, that the innermost shell of all atoms (now called the K shell) has a maximum capacity of two electrons. Hydrogen, with only one electron, has its shell unfilled. Two hydrogen atoms, by pooling and sharing the single electron belonging to each, will mutually fill their shells. This is why hydrogen gas is nearly always found only in the form of the two-atom molecule. Lithium, element number three, has a filled inner shell and one electron in the second, or L shell, which can hold eight electrons. Lithium will readily surrender its L-shell electron so that its filled K shell becomes its outer shell. Fluorine, on the other hand, with seven electrons in its L shell, tends to seize an electron from another atom to complete that shell. Lewis recognized that this phenomenon—the need of every atom to satisfy its outer shell, so to speak—lay at the basis of the chemical behavior of the elements in forming molecules and compounds.

Lewis' history-making paper, "The Atom and the Molecule," is presented here nearly in full. I should explain what he meant by "tautomerism." It had been discovered that some substances behaved as if their molecular structure was not uniform, but varied in different reactions. An example was the organic compound called "isatin." In reactions with some reagents, it exhibited structure I below; in reactions with others, structure II:

Lewis contended, as others had before him, that the molecule might have intermediate forms between these "limiting types."

◆

The Atom and the Molecule [2]

GILBERT N. LEWIS

Molecular Structure

I shall now attempt to show how, by a single type of chemical combination, we may explain the widely varying phenomena of chemical change. With the original assumption of Helmholtz, which has been used by some authors under the name of the electron theory of valence, and according to which a given electron either does or does not pass completely from one atom to another, it is possible to give a very satisfactory explanation of compounds which are of distinctly polar type, but the method becomes less and less satisfactory as we approach the nonpolar type. Great as the difference is between the typical polar and nonpolar substances, we may show how a single molecule may, according to its environment, pass from the extreme polar to the extreme nonpolar form, not *per saltum,* but by imperceptible gradations, as soon as we admit that an electron may be the common property of two atomic shells.

Let us consider first the very polar compounds. Here we find elements with but few electrons in their shells tending to give up these electrons altogether to form positive ions, and elements which already possess a number of electrons tending to increase this number to form the group of eight. Thus Na^+ and Ca^{++} are kernels without a shell, while chloride ion, sulphide ion, nitride ion (as in fused nitrides), may each be represented by an atom having in the shell eight electrons at the corners of a cube.

As an introduction to the study of substances of slightly polar type, we may consider the halogens. In Figure 13–1 I have attempted to show the different forms of the iodine molecule I_2. A

[2] *American Chemical Journal,* Vol. 31 (1916), pp. 772–785.

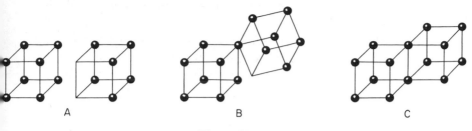

A   B   C

Figure 13–1.

represents the molecule as completely ionized, as it undoubtedly is to a measurable extent in liquid iodine.* Without ionization, we may still have one of the electrons of one atom fitting into the outer shell of the second atom, thus completing its group of eight as in B. But at the same time an electron of the second atom may fit into the shell of the first, thus satisfying both groups of eight and giving the form C, which is the predominant and characteristic structure of the halogens. Now, notwithstanding the symmetry of the form C, if the two atoms are for any reason tending to separate, the two common electrons may cling more firmly sometimes to one of the atoms, sometimes to the other, thus producing some dissymmetry in the molecule as a whole, and one atom will have a slight excess of positive charge, the other of negative. This separation of the charges and the consequent increase in the polar character of the molecule will increase as the atoms become separated to a greater distance until complete ionization results.† Thus between the perfectly symmetrical and nonpolar molecule C and the completely polar and ionized molecule represented by A, there will be an infinity of positions representing a greater or lesser degree of polarity. Now, in a substance like liquid iodine, it must not be assumed that all the

* See Lewis and Wheeler, *Zeitschrift für physikalische Chemie,* Vol. 56 (1906), p. 189.

† When the separation occurs in a nonpolar environment, the atoms may separate in such a way that each retains one of the two common electrons, as in the thermal dissociation of iodine gas.

molecules are in the same state, but rather that some are highly polar, some are almost nonpolar, and others represent all gradations between the two. When we find that iodine in different environments shows different degrees of polarity, it means merely that in one medium there is a larger percentage of the more polar forms. So bromine, although represented by an entirely similar formula, is less polar than iodine. In other words, in the average molecule the separation of the charge is less than in the case of iodine. Chlorine and fluorine are less polar than either and can be regarded as composed almost completely of molecules of the form C.

I wish to emphasize once more the meaning that must be ascribed to the term *tautomerism*. In the simplest case, where we deal with a single tautomeric change, we speak of the two tautomers and sometimes write definite formulas to express the two. But we must not assume that all the molecules of the substance possess either one structure or the other, but rather that these forms represent the two limiting types and that the individual molecules range all the way from one limit to the other. In certain cases where the majority of molecules lie very near to one limit or to the other, it is very convenient and desirable to attempt to express the percentage of the molecules belonging to the one or to the other tautomeric form; but in a case where the majority of molecules lie in the intermediate range and relatively few in the immediate neighborhood of the two limiting forms, such a calculation loses most of its significance.

With the halogens, it is a matter of chance as to which of the atoms acquires a positive and which a negative charge; but in the case of a binary compound composed of different elements, the atoms of one element will be positive in most, though not necessarily all, of the molecules. Thus, in Br_2 the bromine atom is as often positive as negative, but in BrCl it will be usually positive and in IBr usually negative, although in all these substances which are not very polar the separation of charges in the molecule will be slight, whereas in the metallic halides the separation is nearly complete and the halogen atoms acquire almost complete possession of the electrons.

In order to express this idea of chemical union in symbols, I would suggest the use of a colon, or two dots arranged in some other manner, to represent the two electrons which act as the connecting links between the two atoms. Thus we may write Cl_2 as Cl : Cl. If in certain cases we wish to show that one atom in the molecule is on the average negatively charged, we may bring the colon nearer to the negative element. Thus we may write Na :I, and I :Cl. Different spacings to represent different degrees of polarity can, of course, be more freely employed at a blackboard than in type.

It will be noted that, since in the hydrogen-helium row we have the rule of two in the place of the rule of eight, the insertion of one electron into the shell of the hydrogen atom is entirely analogous to the completion of the cube in the case of the halogens. Thus we may consider ordinary hydrogen as a hydride of positive hydrogen in the same sense that chlorine may be regarded as a chloride of positive chlorine. But H_2 is far less polar even than Cl_2. The three main types of hydrogen compounds may be represented therefore by H :Cl, H :H, and Na :H.

We may go further and give a complete formula for each compound by using the symbol of the kernel instead of the ordinary atomic symbol and by adjoining to each symbol a number of dots corresponding to the number of electrons in the atomic shell. Thus we may write

$$H : H, H : \overset{..}{\underset{..}{O}} : H, H : \overset{..}{\underset{..}{I}} :, : \overset{..}{\underset{..}{I}} : \overset{..}{\underset{..}{I}} :,$$

but we shall see that in many cases such a formula represents only one of the numerous extreme tautomeric forms. For the sake of simplicity, we may also use occasionally formulas which show only those electrons concerned in the union of two atoms, as in the preceding paragraphs.

It is evident that the type of union we have so far pictured, although it involves two electrons held in common by two atoms, nevertheless corresponds to the single bond as it is commonly used in graphical formulas. In order to illustrate this point further, we may discuss a problem that has proved extremely embarrassing to a number of theories of valence. I refer to the structure of ammonia and of ammonium ion. Ammonium ion may, of course, on account of the extremely polar character of ammonia and hydrogen ion, be regarded as a loose complex due to the electrical attraction of the two polar molecules. However, as we consider the effect of substituting hydrogen by organic groups, we pass gradually into a field where we may be perfectly certain that four groups are attached directly to the nitrogen atom, and these groups are held with sufficient firmness so that numerous stereochemical isomers have been obtained. The solution of this problem in terms of the theory here presented is extremely simple and satisfactory, and it will be sufficient to write an equation in terms of the new symbols in order to make the explanation obvious. Thus for $NH_3 + H^+ = NH_4^+$ we write

$$H \qquad\qquad\qquad H$$
$$H : \overset{..}{\underset{..}{N}} : + H = H : \overset{..}{\underset{..}{N}} : H \,.$$
$$H \qquad\qquad\qquad H$$

When ammonium ion combines with chloride ion, the latter is not attached directly to the nitrogen but is held simply through electric forces by the ammonium ion.

While the two dots of our formulas correspond to the line that has been used to represent the single bond, we are led through their use to certain formulas of great significance, which I presume would not occur to anyone using the ordinary symbols. Thus, it has been generally assumed that what is known as a bivalent element must be tied by two bonds to another element or elements or remain with an "unsaturated valence." On the other hand, we may now write formulas in which an atom of oxygen is tied by only one pair of electrons to another atom and yet have every element in the compound completely saturated. To illustrate this important point, we may write the formula of perchlorate, sulphate, orthophosphate, and orthosilicate ions, in which each atom has a complete shell of eight electrons. Thus

represents all these ions. If X is Cl, the ion has one negative charge; if S, it has two negative charges; and so on. The union of sulphur trioxide to oxide ion to form sulphate ion is similar to the addition of ammonia and hydrogen ion to form ammonium ion. The acids or acid ions are produced from the above ion by adding hydrogen ion, or H, to the oxygen atoms.

We may next consider the *double bond* in which four electrons are held conjointly by two atoms. Thus Figure 13–2, A, may rep-

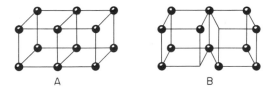

Figure 13–2.

resent the typical structure of the molecule of oxygen. A characteristic feature of the double bond is its tendency to "break." When this happens in a symmetrical way, as it will except in a highly polar environment, it leaves the two atoms concerned in the *odd* state, each with an unpaired electron in the shell. Insofar as a substance with a double bond assumes this other tautomeric form, it will show all the properties of the substances with odd molecules. Thus Figure 13–2, B, represents this tautomeric form of the oxygen molecule; the equilibrium between forms A and B is entirely analogous to the equilibrium between N_2O_4 and NO_2. At low temperatures, almost every known case of combination with oxygen gives first a peroxide. This shows that oxygen exists to an appreciable degree in a form that approximates to the form B, in which it can add directly to other atoms precisely as ethylene forms addition compounds. These two forms of oxygen (which, of course, may merge into one another by continuous gradations) can be represented as

$$\overset{..}{:O}::\overset{..}{O}:$$

and

$$\underset{.\ \ \ \ .}{\overset{..\ \ \ \ ..}{:O:O:}},$$

and the two forms of ethylene as

$$\overset{\displaystyle H \quad H}{\underset{}{H:\overset{..}{C}::\overset{..}{C}:H}}$$

and

$$\overset{\displaystyle H \quad H}{\underset{.\ \ \ .}{H:\overset{..}{C}:\overset{..}{C}:H}}.$$

The instability of multiple bonds and the underlying principle of Baeyer's Strain Theory we shall discuss presently, but before proceeding further in this direction it is important to consider the general relation between the strength of the constraints which hold a molecule together and the stability of the molecule. The term *stability* is used in two very different senses, according as we think of the tendency of a reaction to occur, or the speed of that reaction. We speak of nitric oxide as an extremely stable substance, although it is thermodynamically unstable, and the free energy involved in its decomposition is enormous, but it is so inert that it suffers no appreciable change. A high degree of inertness means ordinarily very rigid constraints operating within the molecule; but these powerful forces may operate only over a very small distance, so that the *work* done in overcoming them may be very small. To illustrate this point, let us consider a piece of iron suspended by a magnet. It is drawn downward by the force of gravity and upward by the magnetic field, and while the net amount of work obtained by separating it from the magnet and allowing it to fall to earth may be positive, it nevertheless will not fall of itself, but can only be drawn from the magnet by a force far greater than that of gravitation. So in the case of the molecule, thermodynamic stability is closely associated with the *work* of breaking some bond, but the inertness of the molecule depends upon the *force* required to break that bond. . . .

In my early theory, the cube was the fundamental structure of all atomic shells. We have seen, however, in the case of elements with lower atomic weights than lithium, that the *pair* of electrons forms the stable group, and we may question whether in general the pair rather than the group of eight should not be regarded as the fundamental unit. Perhaps the chief reasons for assuming the cubical structure were that this is the most symmetrical arrangement of eight electrons and is the one in which the electrons are farthest apart. Indeed, it seems inherently probable that in elements of large atomic shell (large atomic volume) the electrons are sufficiently far from one another so that Coulomb's law of inverse squares is approximately valid, and in such cases it would seem probable that the mutual repulsion of the eight electrons would force them into the cubical structure.

However, this is precisely the kind of a priori reasoning we have decided not to employ in this paper, and when we consider only known chemical phenomena and their best interpretation in terms of atomic structure, we are led to assume a somewhat different arrangement of the group of eight electrons, at least in the case of the more nonpolar substances whose molecules are as a rule composed of atoms of small atomic volume.

The nature of this arrangement is shown in Figure 13–3. The

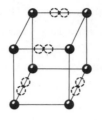

Figure 13–3.

cube representing the electron structure that we have hitherto assumed for the carbon atom is joined to four other atoms, which are not shown in the figure but are attached to the carbon atom each by a pair of electrons. These pairs are indicated by being joined by heavy lines. Assuming now, at least in such very small atoms as that of carbon, that each pair of electrons has a tendency to be drawn together—perhaps by magnetic force if the magneton theory is correct, or perhaps by other forces which become appreciable at small distances—to occupy positions indicated by the dotted circles, we then have a model that is admirably suited to portray all the characteristics of the carbon atom. With the cubical structure, it is impossible not only to represent the triple bond but also to explain the phenomenon of free mobility about a single bond which must always be assumed in stereochemistry. On the other hand, the group of eight electrons in which the *pairs* are symmetrically placed about the center gives identically the model of the tetrahedral carbon atom which has been of such signal utility throughout the whole of organic chemistry.

As usual, two tetrahedra, attached by one, two, or three corners of each, represent, respectively, the single, the double, and the triple bond. In the first case, one pair of electrons is held in common by the two atoms; in the second case, two such pairs; in the third case, three pairs.

The triple bond represents the highest possible degree of union between two atoms. Like a double bond, it may break one bond, producing two *odd* carbon atoms, but it may also break in a way in which the double bond cannot, to leave a single bond and two carbon atoms (bivalent), each of which has a pair of electrons that is not bound to any other atom. The three tautomeric forms may be represented in the case of acetylene by

$$H : C : : : C : H , H : \overset{\cdot}{C} : : \overset{\cdot}{C} : H ,$$

and

$$H : \overset{\cdot\cdot}{C} : \overset{\cdot\cdot}{C} : H .$$

In addition, we have a form corresponding to Nef's acetylidene and such forms as may exist in highly polar media, such as the acetylide ion

$$: C : : : C : H .$$

Let us turn now to a problem in the solution of which the theory that I am presenting shows its greatest serviceability. The electrochemical theories of Davy and Berzelius were overshadowed by the "valence" theory when the attention of chemists was largely drawn to the nonpolar substances of organic chemistry. Of late, the electrochemical theories have come once more into prominence, but there has always been that antagonism between the two views which invariably results when two rival theories are mutually exclusive, while both contain certain elements of truth. Indeed, we may now see that with the interpretation which we are now employing the two theories need not be mutually exclusive, but rather complement one another; for the "valence" theory, which is the classical basis of structural organic chemistry, deals with the fundamental structure of the molecule, while electrochemical considerations show the influence of positive and negative groups in minor distortions of the fundamental form. Let us consider once for all that by a negative element or radical we mean one which tends to draw toward itself the electron pairs which constitute the outer shells of all neighboring atoms and that an electropositive group is one that attracts to a less extent, or repels, these electrons. In the majority of carbon compounds, there is very little of that separation of the charges which gives a compound a polar character, although certain groups, such as hydroxyl, as well as those containing multiple bonds, not only themselves possess a decidedly polar character but increase, according to principles already discussed, the polar character of all neighboring parts of the molecule. However, in such molecules as methane and carbon tetrachloride, instead of assuming, as in some current theory, that four electrons have definitely left hydrogen for carbon in the first case, and carbon for chlorine in the second, we shall consider that in methane there is a slight movement of the charges toward the carbon so that the carbon is slightly charged negatively and that in carbon tetrachloride they are slightly shifted toward the chlorine, leaving the carbon somewhat positive. We must remember that here also we are dealing with averages and that in a few out of many molecules of methane the hydrogen may be negatively charged and the carbon positively.

In a substance like water, the electrons are drawn in from hydrogen to oxygen, and we have in the limiting case a certain number of hydrogen atoms which are completely separated as hydrogen ion. The amount of separation of one of the hydrogen atoms, and therefore the degree of ionization, will change very greatly when the other hydrogen atom is substituted by a positive or negative group. As a familiar example, we may consider acetic acid, in which one hydrogen is replaced by chlorine, $H_2ClCCOOH$. The electrons, being drawn toward the chlorine, permit the pair of electrons joining the methyl and carboxyl groups to approach nearer to the methyl carbon. This pair of electrons, exercising therefore a smaller repulsion upon the other electrons of the hydroxyl oxygen, permit these also to shift in the same direction. In other words, all the electrons move toward the left, producing a greater separation of the electrons from the hydrogen of the hydroxyl, and thus a stronger acid. This simple explanation is applicable to a vast number of individual cases. It need only be borne in mind that although the effect of such a displacement of electrons at one end of a chain proceeds throughout the whole chain, it becomes less marked the greater the distance and the more rigid the constraints which hold the electrons in the intervening atoms.

◆

14

THERMODYNAMICS
AND AFFINITY

The term *thermodynamics* was retained long after it had been extended from the dynamics of thermal energy to all forms of energy. For chemists, the central theme was the involvement of affinity in these changes. The author of our next adventure, Walther Nernst (1864–1941), wrote a textbook of theoretical chemistry "from the standpoint of Avogadro's theory and thermodynamics"; he was twenty-nine when its first edition was published (1893).

About ten years later, he began to develop a new aspect of thermodynamics. He had a deep feeling for the position of this work in the flow of history up to his time. It will be appropriate to take a brief look at some events in this history.

Models and mathematics mark the paths to modern chemistry. Atomists of the seventeenth century, such as Gassendi and Lémery, saw the atoms equipped with points and edges, with hooks and eyes. John Dalton had actual models of atoms made of wood to visualize their connections to molecules. From 1850

184

on, chemists and physicists introduced differential equations for the factors that determine the course of a chemical reaction. The graphic formulas of Kekulé were the projected outlines of models. J. H. van't Hoff and G. N. Lewis used both models and mathematics in representing idealizations of reality. They arrived at these idealizations by going to limits where reality, so to say, was just beginning to be loaded with all those manifold influences that science could handle only one by one at first, eventually trying to piece them together again.

Sadi Carnot and Josiah Willard Gibbs followed this approach to reality by way of limit states. Mathematics provided specific rules about how to reach and define the states at the limits where one or the other special factor had extreme values, zero or infinity.

Nernst set out to explore a different kind of limit state. To the two principles of thermodynamics he added a third one, defining what happens to entropy at the approach to the absolute zero of temperature.

This was not the first time that a third principle had been proposed. In 1867, and, after extensive experimentation on thermochemistry, in 1878, Marcelin Berthelot had declared it as a general law "that every chemical reaction leads to the production of those substances that develop the maximum amount of heat." Essentially, this principle declared a tendency of all chemical change, and it was thus in the same class with the principle of Le Châtelier, which, however, did not claim the rank of a third thermodynamic principle.

Nernst discussed Berthelot's principle in the first edition of his *Theoretische Chemie* in 1893. He pointed out that the principle would be true only if the heat of reaction was independent of the temperature. He continued:

Since every chemical process, like any natural process at all, without the introduction of outside energy can go only in the direction in which it is able to furnish external work, and since furthermore any measure of chemical affinity has to fulfill the absolute condition that every process must go in the direction of the affinity, we need not hesitate to define the maximal external work of a chemical process ("change of free energy") as the measure of affinity.[1]

From the new law for the approach to the absolute zero, Nernst arrived at experiments and calculations for normal conditions in about the same manner as van't Hoff proceeded from the idea of ideal solutions of substances to a new understanding of real solutions, at least those in which the concentrations were relatively low.

The following excerpts are translated from the German.

◆

Thermodynamic Calculation of Chemical Affinities [2]

WALTHER NERNST

General Comments

Among the various changes in energy, those that are associated with the course of chemical processes have always been conspicuous because of their magnitude. Therefore, the application of classical thermodynamics to processes of this type has met with particular success. Nowadays, no intensive investigation of a chemical equilibrium is regarded as complete if it does not make use of the two main laws of heat theory.

To be sure, a purely thermodynamic approach will never be entirely satisfactory, if only because the question of reaction velocity is entirely outside its field; and one will always have to make sure that, in addition to thermodynamics, the principles of atomistics are included. Atomistics has explained a number of processes in an entirely satisfactory manner, especially in the

[1] Walther Nernst, *Theoretische Chemie* (Stuttgart: Enke, 1893), p. 543.
[2] *Berichte der Deutschen Chemischen Gesellschaft,* Vol. 47 (1914), pp. 608–635.

form of the kinetic theory of gases, as, for example, the work done by a gas in its expansion, or the transfer of heat through a gas. But if we ask about the accomplishments of atomistics in the mechanical explanation of chemical processes, we must admit openly that everything that has so far been attempted in this field has not only remained incomplete but must be considered basically faulty.

Certainly the explanation of the law of constant and multiple proportions and the marvelous systematics, especially of organic compounds, are tremendous achievements of atomistics purely in the field of chemistry; but these applications are not of a mechanical nature and have hardly any relation to the manner in which two atoms combine in a compound, with the magnitude of the forces that enter in, and with the change in energy thus determined. Not only in chemical processes, but also in the probably simpler phenomena of steam formation, fusion, and the transformation of various modifications, the same gap exists.

The principal fault in the ideas considered up to now seems to lie in the fact that, for example, in the consideration of steam formation, one simply calculated the work to be done in the dislocation of a molecule of liquid from the interior of the liquid phase into the gaseous space, using the theory of potentials. This formulation is questionable, however, because even a small change in the state of motion of the molecule can undoubtedly exert a great effect under certain conditions; but we do not know how this is to be taken into account—a fact which, of course, cannot justify the silent neglect that has generally been practiced up to now.

Of no lesser significance is a second circumstance that plays a decisive role specifically in the chemical processes themselves, for, as Planck * has shown, the laws of mechanics undergo a thorough transformation if one is dealing with the motion of atoms about their resting position. Here, also, we can only say at

* See the discussion of Planck's quantum theory in Chapter 8, above. (Ed.)

this time that the neglect of Planck's quantum theory (or perhaps of any other, future theory which also leads to Planck's radiation formula) had to place the stamp of incompleteness on all previous attempts at explaining chemical processes mechanically. Certainly, we do not know yet how the new views should be taken into account in this matter; nevertheless, we have made progress in being able to state with certainty now: Something mysterious is hidden within the laws of atom mechanics which is explained in part by radiation theory, in part by the more recent studies of specific heats, and which apparently must be thoroughly understood before a mechanical treatment of chemical processes will be possible. Thus, we know, for example, that the laws of motion of a double star are quite different from those of a diatomic gas, and we can at least indicate broadly in what sense the laws of pure mechanics are modified in the second case.

There is only one temperature point at which we can probably use the laws of mechanics safely; namely, when the motion of the atoms has completely stopped, i.e., at absolute zero temperature. Without doubt the laws of ordinary potential theory can be applied here; the heat formation that corresponds to the dislocation of the atoms from one state (e.g., in the form of free elements) to another state (e.g., in the form of a chemical combination) can be regarded as the equivalent of the forces exerted here; in other words, at absolute zero the chemical affinity must be equal to the heat formation.

Now, the second heat law gives quite a general relation between the maximum work A, which we previously designated as the sum of all forces produced in the chemical process under consideration and to which we shall refer below, as usual, briefly as "chemical affinity," * and the heat developed, U:

$$A - U = T \frac{dA}{dT}. \qquad (1)$$

* Undoubtedly it is more practical to define chemical affinity by the so-called "thermodynamic potential," but in our considerations this does not make any noticeable difference.

Since we observed above that the left side of the equation disappears at absolute zero, we can write:

$$\lim \left(T \frac{dA}{dT} \right) = O \text{ for } T = O .$$

But, according to this equation, even at $T = O$, dA/dT (its negative value is also called "entropy") can still possess a finite value and can even be infinitely large; it must, however, be of less than first order.

Equation (1) contains the complete application of the two heat laws to chemical processes; as has been shown especially by Helmholtz, all that the older thermodynamics was able to teach can be demonstrated clearly by means of it. Therefore it will be useful to go into it a little more thoroughly.

U can be looked up in thermochemical tables for room temperature, and we now want to refer to the well-known law that U can be calculated for arbitrary other temperatures from the specific heats.

A can essentially be determined by two methods, both of which were already used by Helmholtz; namely, by measurement of the chemical equilibrium or of the electromotive force.

Of course, dA/dT can then be found by measuring A at two slightly different temperatures.

Historical Background

Under such circumstances, the desire to derive A thermodynamically beyond equation (1) appeared quite early. The first determined effort in this direction came from Julius Thomsen, if one disregards Helmholtz' method of calculating the electromotive force of galvanic elements, which will be discussed further below. Thomsen, in his "Contributions to a Thermochemical System," emphasized repeatedly as early as 1852 that strong manifestations of chemical affinity are accompanied by intense heat formation and that chemical processes associated with heat absorption occur only rarely. He therefore arrived at the following conclusion:

"When a body falls, it develops a certain mechanical effect that is proportionate to its weight and to the space traversed. In chemical processes that take place in the usual direction, a certain effect likewise appears; but it shows itself in this instance as heat formation. The heat formation constitutes a measure of the chemical force developed in the process."

We have seen above that a chemical process may not be regarded—at least not above absolute zero—as a phenomenon of attraction, comparable to the falling of a stone; but we shall not hold this against Thomsen, in view of the fact that attempts to use this interpretation are still being made repeatedly today in spite of the kinetic theory of heat. Furthermore, Thomsen himself already recognized the untenability of the above concept in the early seventies, probably influenced chiefly by the results of his very ingenious method for determining the affinity between acids and bases.

We know that the same law was formulated in 1869 by the second master of thermochemistry, Berthelot, and energetically defended by him for a long time. Berthelot's formulation is the following:

"Every chemical transformation which takes place without the interposition of a foreign energy aims toward the production of that substance or that system of substances which develops the most heat."

Both formulations—the older one by Thomsen, as well as the later one by Berthelot—lead one to set $A = U$ in formula (1) for all temperatures. It is unnecessary to give the reasons for the inadmissibility of this equation again in more detail, but a reference to a remark by Horstmann will be useful for further clarification. According to him, the proof of chemical equilibrium or, what amounts to the same thing, of a reversible reaction was sufficient for refuting Berthelot's principle. Since the reaction takes place in one or the other sense, depending on the ratio of quantities of the reacting components, on one or the other side of the equilibrium, the reaction in the vicinity of chemical equilibrium must proceed in one instance according to Berthelot's principle with heat formation and in the other, certainly in opposition to that principle, with heat absorption.

We have emphasized above that the electromotive force of a galvanic element is proportional to the affinity of the process providing the current. The Thomsen-Berthelot principle, then, can also be expressed in such a way that the electromotive force of galvanic elements would have to be proportional to the heat formed per electrochemical gram element. It is of historical interest to emphasize that this formulation is found already in the famous paper by Helmholtz on the conservation of energy (1847). The method of calculation, which was only indicated there, was later carried out by William Thomson for several examples. More intensive study has shown, in agreement with our earlier observations, that one can indeed frequently calculate the electromotive force of galvanic elements very accurately from the heat formed, especially in cases where the affinity is strong, but that one may in no way speak of a strict law.

It is evident that all further progress must be tied to equation (1); a relationship must be found that is independent of the special nature of the reaction under consideration, if the uncertainty inherent in equation (1) is to be overcome.

For a certain class of reactions—namely, those where a gas is formed from one or more solid substances—Le Châtelier, Matignon, and Forcrand found the following approximate relationship: if Q designates the heat formed at constant pressure, and T', the absolute temperature at which the dissociation pressure of the gas being formed equals atmospheric pressure, then:

$$\frac{Q}{T'} = \text{approx. } 32 .$$

In this case, disregarding the variation of Q with temperature, the second heat law gives

$$\ln p = -\frac{Q}{RT} + \text{const.}$$

We recognize immediately that Le Châtelier–Matignon's rule gives a value of approximately 32 for the undetermined integration constant multiplied by R. This rule is only approximately valid; nevertheless, it provides an important cue, and it probably deserved more attention than it was given formerly. We shall become acquainted with a more precise formulation later on.

Van't Hoff set up an equation in 1904 that was hardly satisfactory. If one wants to satisfy the effect of temperature on U by the (seemingly!) simplest equation:

$$U = U_0 + \alpha T, \qquad (2)$$

integrating (1) gives

$$A = U_0 + aT + \alpha T \ln T, \qquad (3)$$

where a is the constant of integration. Van't Hoff assumed that a was small. This hypothesis is not only arbitrary but also evidently inaccurate. For, even if we assume the case that a equals zero, we only need to alter the temperature scale—i.e., divide the space between the melting and boiling points of water into a million instead of a hundred parts—and we immediately have a finite and even sizable value for a. It is hardly likely that the natural laws are guided by the fact that Celsius divided the above-mentioned temperature interval into a hundred parts and that he happened to choose water as the standard substance.

The earlier attempts to go beyond equation (1) thus were unsuccessful; but at least the problem had been sharply formulated. The clearest position taken, next to Helmholtz, was probably that of Le Châtelier as early as in 1888. I want to reproduce his words here: *

* *Les équilibres chimiques* (Paris, 1888), p. 184.

"It is very probable that the integration constant, like the other coefficients of the differential equation, is a definite function of certain physical properties of the reacting substances. The determination of the nature of the function would lead to complete knowledge of the laws of equilibrium. Independently of new experimental data, it would determine a priori the complete equilibrium conditions which correspond to a given chemical reaction; up to now, it has not been possible to determine the exact nature of this constant."

If I may now discuss my part in the solution of the problem, it seemed noteworthy to me from the beginning that, for an erroneous law of nature, Berthelot's rule still is too frequently applicable to be ignored entirely, and therefore I had already emphasized in the first edition of my textbook of theoretical chemistry (1893) "that it is quite possible that Berthelot's principle, in a clearer form, may at some time again become important." It was particularly noticeable that for solid substances, affinity and heat formation frequently coincide. It was clear from the beginning, on the other hand, that the identification of these two magnitudes actually becomes meaningless for gaseous systems, for the maximum work depends on the initial and final concentrations of the reacting gases, while the heat formation is entirely independent of these. Thus, the question arose whether a relationship between heat formation and chemical equilibrium could be found empirically, at least for comparable reactions such as:

$$Cl_2 + H_2 = 2HCl$$
$$2NO = N_2 + O_2$$

or:

$$2H_2 + O_2 = 2H_2O$$
$$2CO + O_2 = 2CO_2$$
$$3O_2 = 2O_3 \, .$$

Therefore, together with a large number of collaborators, and guided by such considerations, about ten years ago I undertook the determination of equilibriums in gases, on which only very little, and usually uncertain, observed material was previously available.

Thermodynamic Considerations

In its application to gaseous systems, the second heat law leads to the following result. Experience teaches us that the specific heats vary only slowly with temperature, so that it is suitable and convenient, to begin with, to assume an expression of the form

$$c = c_0 + aT + bT^2 + \ldots \qquad (4)$$

to be valid; c_0 would thus be the specific heat at very low temperatures.

Furthermore, since, according to a law by Kirchhoff, the temperature dependence of the heat of reaction U is determined by the specific heats of the substances participating in the reaction, we can also set

$$U = U_0 + \alpha T + \beta T^2 + \gamma T^3 + \ldots, \qquad (5)$$

where U_0 is the heat of reaction near absolute zero.

Substituting in the equation of the reaction isochore

$$U = RT^2 \frac{d \ln K}{dT} \qquad (6)$$

and integrating, we easily find

$$\ln K = -\frac{U_0}{RT} + \frac{\alpha}{R} \ln T + \frac{\beta}{R} T + \frac{\gamma}{2R} T^2 + \ldots + I \qquad (7)$$

where I is the constant of integration.

The right-hand side of equation (7) thus contains, besides the constant of integration, only pure thermal magnitudes (heat of reaction, specific heat, or, respectively, its temperature coefficients); but the second heat law says nothing at all about the integration constant itself.

At very low temperatures, the effect of all other members disappears, and we obtain

$$RT \ln K = -U_0 ,$$

i.e., we can here calculate the equilibrium from the heat of reaction U_0; at finite temperatures, however, first the effect of $\alpha T \ln T$ and RTI, and then also that of the remaining members will be noticeable.

From the experimental point of view, we arrive at the problem that the behavior of gases cannot be measured at lower temperatures because they cease to remain capable of existing in significant concentrations.

If we now consider the opposite of gaseous equilibrium—namely, a reaction between solid substances only—a limiting transition to absolute zero seems entirely possible in theoretical as well as experimental respects. And here it is noticeable that Berthelot's principle frequently fits quite well, especially if one is dealing with relatively great reaction heats. Thus, the conjecture forced itself upon me (1906) that this is a matter of a limiting law of such a kind that A and U not only become equal at absolute zero but approach each other asymptotically. Thus we should have:

$$\lim \frac{dA}{dT} = \lim \frac{dU}{dT} \text{ (for } T = 0) ; \qquad (8)$$

but it is to be noted that the above equation is applicable, to begin with, only to pure solid or liquid substances; at absolute zero, gases stop being capable of existing, and the behavior of solutions must still be investigated more closely.

We recognize further that equation (8) combined with (1) gives

$$\lim \frac{dA}{dT} = O, \quad \lim \frac{dU}{dT} = O \; (\text{for } T = O) \, .$$

The relationship

$$\lim \frac{dU}{dT} = O \; (\text{for } T = O)$$

teaches us that the atomic heats of the elements and compounds must be strictly additive at low temperatures; already in the first practical applications of my theorem I was led to the conjecture that all of them must converge toward very small values at low temperatures. The experimental and theoretical studies of recent times have, as we know, not only confirmed this conjecture but even made it into a certainty that the specific heats of all solid substances converge toward zero at low temperatures.

We shall make use of this below, and we shall find the following equation to be strictly valid for low temperatures, if we include the very important result that was confirmed theoretically by Debye and experimentally by Eucken and, quite recently, also by Schwers and myself, that the specific heat changes in proportion to the third power of the absolute temperature at low temperatures:

$$U = U_0 + \delta T^4, \quad A = U_0 - \frac{\delta}{3} T^4 \, . \tag{14}$$

In the discussion of the following examples, we shall limit ourselves to a graphic representation, and I shall give references to the appropriate publications for the specific numerical material. It is even quite possible and, in many cases, practicable, to determine the relationship between affinity and heat of reaction by purely graphic means.

We shall assume, for example, that the heat of reaction was measured for a single arbitrary temperature and that we know the specific heats of the reacting solid substances down to very low temperatures. By assuming the T^3 law for the very low temperatures that are inaccessible to measurement, we are then in a position to draw the heat of reaction as a function of temperature with great accuracy down to absolute zero.

The integral of the equation

$$A - U = T \frac{dA}{dT} \tag{1}$$

is

$$A = -T \int_0^T \frac{U}{T^2} \, dT + cT ; \tag{15}$$

for $T = O$, we have

$$A = U_0 ;$$

i.e., as was already mentioned, Berthelot's law is valid here without restriction. However, for higher temperatures the value of the integration constant c becomes decisive, and the second heat law leaves this value undetermined.

Figure 14–1 shows this. The solid curve U represents the dependence of the heat formed on the absolute temperature; thus

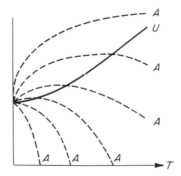

Figure 14–1. Rhombic S → Monoclinic S. The change of $U = $ total energy and $A = $ free energy in accordance with the formulas:
$$U = 1.57 + 1.15 \times T^2; \quad A = 1.57 - 1.15 \times T^2.$$
abscissae $= T$; ordinate $= $ cal. (After Nernst.)

U_0 is the value this quantity assumes at absolute zero; then each of the dotted curves A is a solution of the above equation, and one sees at once that there is no point, and therefore no value for A, through which we could not draw an A curve out of the entire set of curves. In other words, every arbitrary value of the affinity A is compatible with any experimentally given shape of the heat formation, so that the second heat law abandons us here to a large extent. It gives us a precise answer only for absolute zero, since the curves for heat formation and affinity intersect here so that both quantities become identical, as Berthelot had assumed to be the case for all temperatures.

But if we now include the new heat law, the A curve must run parallel to the U curve at absolute zero; in other words, from the infinite set of A curves one, and only one, is fixed as being possible.

If we wish to determine it, not by calculation from equation (15), in which c must be set equal to zero according to the new law, but by purely graphic means, we must first, starting at abso-

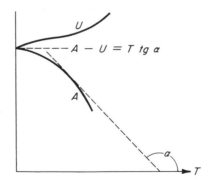

Figure 14–2. After Nernst.

lute zero, draw it parallel to the U curve; the further direction is given at every point by the equation

$$\tan\alpha = \frac{dA}{dT} = \frac{A - U}{T}.$$

With some practice, the A curve can be drawn quickly and with sufficient accuracy in this way.

Examples of Condensed Systems

In condensed systems, also, Berthelot's principle sometimes fails completely; in particular, at the melting point and at the transformation point the affinity equals zero because the two phases in question are here in equilibrium, while the heat formed (heat of fusion or, respectively, heat of transformation) can even have considerable values. The application of the new heat law thus leads in this instance to especially characteristic consequences, the influence of the specific heats, which had formerly not been sufficiently recognized, proving decisive for the position of the melting or transformation point. As an example, let us look at the transformation of sulphur.

Transformation of Sulphur Different authors have measured the heat of transformation of rhombic into monosymmetric sulphur, the maximum work to be obtained in this and the specific heats for both modifications; in addition, the temperature of the transformation point is known exactly.[*] It turned out that, with the aid of the simple formulas

$$U = 1.57 + 1.15.10^{-5}T^2$$
$$A = 1.57 - 1.15.10^{-5}T^2,$$

all observations can be reproduced almost within the accuracy of the errors of observation.

The accompanying curve (Figure 14–3) gives a picture that approaches reality still more closely; here, the U curve is drawn from the available thermal measurements and the A curve is determined graphically as described above. The latter is in agree-

[*] For details cf. Nernst, *Zeitschrift für Elektrochemie*, Vol. 15 (1909), pp. 736–737.

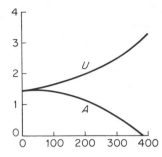

Figure 14–3. After Nernst.

ment with the available measurements to the extent allowed by the accuracy of the available thermal measurements; since the very small difference of the specific heats of the two modifications of sulphur determines the course of the U curve, it can, of course, be indicated only within a certain accuracy. But it can probably be considered definite, and it is this alone that we are concerned with, that the two curves are tangent to each other, in agreement with the new heat law.

Combination of Water of Crystallization   In recent times,[*] the reaction

$$CuSO_4 + H_2O = CuSO_4,H_2O$$

has been investigated very intensively. The quantities measured were the heat of hydration with liquid water, the dissociation potentials at higher temperatures, and the specific heats of the two salts and of ice down to very low temperatures (Figure 14–4).

With the aid of the second heat law, it was then possible to calculate the dissociation potential π also for the ordinary zero temperature point; if p is the vapor pressure of ice at this temperature, it is found that

$$A = RT \ln \frac{p}{\pi} = 4{,}415 \text{ cal}.$$

[*] A. Siggel, *Zeitschrift für Elektrochemie*, Vol. 19 (1913), p. 341.

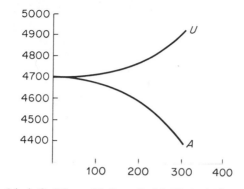

Figure 14–4. $CuSO_2 + H_2O = CuSO_4H_2O$. (After Nernst.)

On the other hand, with the aid of the new heat law, using the heat formed in this reaction at the same temperature (4,910 cal) and using the specific heats, the result was:

$$A = 4,475 \text{ cal},$$

in satisfactory agreement with the value above. Finally, for absolute zero, it was calculated that

$$A_0 = U_0 = 4,680 \text{ cal},$$

and it can be seen (as seems to be most frequently the case) that U increases with temperature while A decreases; but the latter quantity would cross the temperature axis only at such high temperatures that the ice would have long ceased to exist and that, in practice, a point of transformation is therefore not present.

Such a process will always occur if the molecular heat of the water of crystallization is smaller than that of ice; potassium ferrocyanide, which crystallizes with three moles of water, is an example of the reverse case. The accompanying diagram (Figure 14–5)* shows the energy relationships, which are very peculiar

* Schottky, *Zeitschrift für physikalische Chemie,* Vol. 64 (1908), p. 441; W. Nernst, *Berichte der Berliner Akademie* (1910), p. 277.

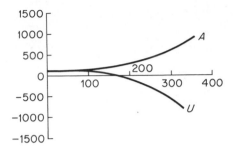

Figure 14–5. $K_4Fe(CN)_6 + 3H_2O = K_4Fe(CN)_6, 3H_2O$. (After Nernst.)

here; one sees that U becomes O at $T = 160$, and that U becomes negative at higher temperatures, while A remains positive and even increases.

Thus, we may probably say in summary that it has been possible to test the new heat law on a very extensive and varied group of facts, numerous chemical equilibriums having been calculated from thermal data or from the combination of thermal data and vapor-pressure measurements.

Independent of this, it may also be derived, as I was unable to do in detail here, from a fact established by very many measurements done in recent times according to which the specific heats of solid and liquid substances assume vanishingly small values at very low temperatures.

Third, as Mr. Planck recently explained here, it is closely related to the theory of energy quanta, and thus even the phenomena of heat radiation, strange as this may sound at first, give support to our law from an entirely different direction.

◆

15

CATALYSIS

The close connection, if not identity, of affinity with electricity had been the basic assumption in the work of Berzelius, who in 1835 defined affinity as "the force that always acts between electrically polar components." However, at that time apparent exceptions to the rule of affinity had been found. When the number of exceptions to a rule increases, they have to be recognized as establishing the need for a new rule. Berzelius invented one and gave it the name "catalysis." He selected this word to form a counterpart to analysis. "Catalysis" would include those instances in which "simple or complex substances in solid or dissolved form have the property of exerting an influence that is quite different from the usual chemical affinity by causing a reaction without taking part in it themselves, although this may occasionally also happen."[1]

Berzelius talked about a "catalytic force," but he formed no theory concerning its way of acting. Had he tried to do so, he would have had to discuss the contradiction that was here in-

[1] Jacob Berzelius, Jahres-Bericht über die Fortschritte der physikalisch-chemischen Wissenschaften, No. 15. Tübingen: Henrich Lapp, 1836, p. 537 (presented to the Swedish Academy of Science, March 31, 1835).

volved. What relationship did catalysts have to the reagents whose reactions they promoted? Did not the concept of affinity embrace all types of relationships between substances?

While the nature of catalytic action remained dark and unexplored, the use of catalysis was greatly extended during the following decades. Berzelius had predicted that thousands of catalytic reactions would be found, and he was right. Through the study of some of these reactions, Wilhelm Ostwald (1853–1932) arrived at an improved formulation for the principle of catalysis at the end of the century. Prominent among the topics of his investigation was esterification, to which Berthelot had devoted so much of his efforts.

Ostwald's definition of catalysis was later completed by his former student, Alwin Mittasch, who included the selective or directional effect. The following report has been translated from the German.

◆

Catalysis [2]

WILHELM OSTWALD

The phenomena summarized by Berzelius are the following: the transformation, discovered in 1811 by Kirchhoff, of starch into dextrin and sugar by boiling with dilute acids; the same effect of malt extract, also demonstrated by him in 1813; the partial isolation, carried out in 1833 by Payen and Persoz, of the substance that is active in this process, namely, diastase; the decomposition, investigated in 1818 by Thenard, of hydrogen peroxide by metals, oxides, and by fibrin; the effect of platinum on combustible gas mixtures (J. Davy, 1817, and Döbereiner, 1822); and finally, as a result of the above-mentioned experiment by Mitscherlich, the formation of ether.

[2] *Zeitschrift für Elektrochemie,* Vol. 7 (1901), pp. 995–1003.

These processes have in common that they are brought about by the presence of substances whose components do not appear in the end products and which therefore are not used up in the reaction. Accordingly, Berzelius defines them as follows: *"The catalytic power essentially appears to consist in the fact that substances are capable, by their mere presence and not by their affinity, of eliciting the affinities which are dormant at this temperature, so that, because of them, the elements within a composite substance arrange themselves in other relationships by which greater electrochemical neutralization is produced."*

Catalyses in Homogeneous Mixtures

. . . The group of contact effects to be discussed now is the largest and most important theoretically. Most of the innumerable catalytic effects discovered in the intervening time belong in this category.

If we ask whether the explanation given for the first case is applicable here, also, the answer must be negative. The essential feature in the first case was the occurrence of the new phase; but this is excluded here by the definition.

We find the correct point of view for the new problem if we adhere to the general condition that has just been postulated for all systems that are subject to a contact effect; it shall not represent a stable state, for such a state cannot experience any change without the addition of energy. But what is the behavior of unstable structures when they are homogeneous?

The answer is that homogeneous, unstable structures (i.e., assemblies of substances) cannot exist other than in a state of transformation. A supersaturated solution can, if the supersaturation remains within certain limits, be stored with appropriate safeguards for an unlimited time, and no change will occur in it. However, a liquid that, without the addition of free energy, can yield other liquid products that remain in solution cannot be stored without forming these products. This may take place extremely slowly—so slowly that no change can be demonstrated at all without prolonged special study directed toward this purpose. But the most reliable foundations known to us for general conclusions—namely, the energy laws—demand that the transformation actually take place. They dictate no numerical value for the speed that must be maintained in the process; they only require that this speed shall not be strictly zero, but have a finite value.

In this way, we at once obtain the definition of a catalyst for this case, also: *"A catalyst is any substance which, without appearing in the end product of a chemical reaction, alters its speed."*

The first theory of catalytic phenomena was formulated by Liebig for the purpose of making the concept created by Berzelius appear superfluous. Liebig conceived of catalysis as a direct consequence of the mechanical law of inertia. His statement says: *"This cause is the capacity, possessed by a substance engaged in decomposition or combination, i.e., in chemical action, of eliciting in another substance in contact with it the same chemical activity, or making it capable of undergoing the same change which it experiences itself.* This capacity is best exemplified by a burning substance (one engaged in action) through which we elicit the same activity in other substances by bringing them near the burning one."

Obviously, Liebig's explanation was rather unfortunate. His own example defeats him, for to ignite something one does not need a burning substance, but merely a hot one; it is entirely irrelevant for the result whether it is hot due to a chemical process or for any other reason (e.g., due to an electric current). Such objections were indeed raised, and Liebig had cause to formulate his hypothesis differently. He explained his view in the following words in connection with the question of the fermentation of sugar:

"Heat is capable of eliminating the static moment in the elements of many chemical combinations. Similarly, this occurs by means of a substance whose elements are themselves in a state

of eliminated equilibrium; the motion in which its atoms are engaged is imparted to the atoms of the elements of sugar; they no longer remain in the state in which they form sugar, but order themselves according to their special affinities." . . .

That the whole matter actually had entered a dead-end track because of the hypothesis of molecular vibrations is seen from the fact that the problem which, at one time, had been treated with such great zeal did not subsequently become the subject of any sustained scientific study. For a long time, only isolated investigators concerned themselves with catalytic phenomena, observing and describing them. Schönbein, to whose investigations we owe so many of the facts that we know at this time, did not participate in the theoretical disputes about their causes; instead, it was an evident pleasure for him to pursue these phenomena which contemporary chemistry, for which he had little regard, did not explain or classify.

Another thought that had been postulated much earlier but had not gained acceptance for a long time presents a much more favorable picture. This is the idea of intermediary reactions.

It had its origin in the first scientific treatment given the chemical reactions in a lead chamber during the sulphuric acid process. In an investigation which has remained a classic, Clément and Desormes, in 1806, provided the explanation that is still generally accepted today for the effect that the oxides of nitrogen have in the oxidation of sulphurous acid by the oxygen in air. As all of you know, this is based on the assumption that sulphurous acid is oxidized by the higher oxides of nitrogen, while these are transformed into nitrogen. The latter again combines with the oxygen of the air, and the reaction can again take place. Thus, a small quantity of nitrogen oxides serves to oxidize unlimited quantities of sulphurous acid.

It is strange that this case was not even discussed at the time of the dispute between Berzelius and Liebig. It was not until later that applications of the old point of view were found to other cases in which chemical reactions are accelerated by certain auxiliary substances, although there is no stoichiometric relationship with these. But gradually this concept became more and more widespread, and today it must be regarded as the oldest and most important attempt to explain certain, though perhaps not all, catalytic processes. . . .

Assuming that the appropriateness of the theory of intermediary products has been demonstrated in individual cases (this will happen, according to all indications), a new question now arises; namely, whether this provides an explanation of all catalytic processes. I believe that the answer to this must be an unconditional no. I believe that I know a considerable number of catalytic processes to which such an explanation is not applicable. In particular, I see no possibility that the delaying catalytic effect could be explained by means of intermediary products. If a reaction proceeds more slowly through the intermediary products than in the direct way, it will take place by the latter, and the possible existence of intermediary products has no effect whatever on the process. . . .

A more complicated case of catalytic phenomena is that of processes in which the substances participating in the reaction have an additional catalytic effect themselves. Among the available possibilities of autocatalysis, I only want to mention the case in which an accelerator may be created by the reaction itself. For example, this occurs in one of the best-known reactions, the solution of metals in nitric acid. The nitrous acid thus produced greatly accelerates the velocity of action of the nitric acid, and thus the following phenomenon comes about:

If the metal is placed in pure acid, the reaction begins extremely slowly. As it progresses, it becomes faster and finally violent. When this period has passed, the process slows down and ends with a velocity converging toward zero.

This is in noticeable contrast to the usual course of reactions, which start with the maximal velocity and, because of the gradual consumption of the effective substances, become progressively slower.

In this connection, physiological analogies intrude irresistibly; this is a typical characteristic of fever. And still another important physiological fact can be illustrated in the same way: habit and memory. I have here two samples of the same nitric acid, which differ only in the fact that I previously dissolved a small piece of copper in one of them. I now introduce two identical sheets of copper into the two acids, which are standing in the same water container so that they have the same temperature. You can see at once that the acid that had already dissolved copper has become "accustomed" to this work and starts to carry it out very skillfully and quickly, while the inexperienced acid does not know what to do with the copper and executes its action so sluggishly and awkwardly that we cannot wait for it. That this is a case of catalysis by nitrous acid becomes evident when I add some sodium nitrite to the sluggish acid: here, too, the copper is at once attacked and dissolved.

Heterogeneous Catalysis

The best-known case of heterogeneous catalysis is the effect of platinum on combustible gas mixtures. Previously, the phenomena occurring in detonating gas were of prime interest; now, for practical reasons, the combustion of sulphur dioxide into trioxide has become the most important.

All these cases, also, probably involve accelerations of slow reactions, even though it has to be admitted that in detonating gas, for example, the formation of water at ordinary temperatures without a catalyst has not yet been demonstrated.

But the steadiness of the change in velocity with the temperature in this case justifies us in assuming that there is indeed a very low reaction speed even at ordinary temperatures. That it is so particularly low is in keeping with the general fact that all reactions of gases take place at a relatively very low speed.

This important fact is clearly evident, for example, in the experiments of Berthelot and Péan de Saint-Gilles. A comparison of ester formation from acid and alcohol at the same temperature was made in two experiments, the substances used being liquid in one case and gaseous in the other. The experiments do not lend themselves to precise calculations; but the question is not whether the slowing down can be completely explained by the great decrease of concentrations or whether (as is more likely) there is a more significant meaning; it is sufficient to know that the reaction velocity was depressed to about a thousandth by the transition into gaseous form.

It is possible to use this as a basis for a theory of the above-mentioned accelerations (Bodenstein). If we imagine that, at the existing temperature, a part of the gaseous system is transformed into the liquid state, or if we assume a density corresponding to this state, the reaction will occur more rapidly in this portion, and the liquid components of the initial substances will be transformed into the end products. Now, if the liquefying or compressing agent is so constituted that it compresses new quantities of the initial substances after the first compressed portion is used up, then these again will react quickly, and so on; the result is an acceleration of the reaction. Such an effect on the gases due to platinum is quite possible.

I do not want to assert with this explanation that platinum catalyses actually take place in this way, but only wish to point out that there is a possible way in which they could occur. We then would have the simplest and purest case of the accelerating intermediary reaction, to which I have referred earlier.

As Professor [Georg] Bredig explained to me verbally a short time ago, the mechanism of such an acceleration can be made clear in terms of a liquid medium in which small amounts of another liquid are suspended. If this suspended liquid has such a property that the reaction of the substances present occurs more quickly in it than in the main mass, the components of the reagents present there would be transformed first. The product would diffuse into the surrounding liquid; likewise, new amounts of the reagents would enter, since the concentration of the different substances always becomes uniform by diffusion. In this way, the entire amount of reagents would gradually make its way through the suspended liquid and react there; the result is an acceleration of the reaction.

The material presented here can perhaps also be applied, according to Bredig, to the case in which the catalyst is present in the liquid in the colloidal state. As is well known, Professor Bredig and his students, in a series of excellent experiments, have demonstrated and measured a great variety of the most energetic catalytic effects that can be produced by colloidal platinum that he made and by other colloidal metals. He has also emphasized repeatedly that the catalysts that occur naturally and are so very effective—namely, the enzymes—likewise are in a state of colloidal solution or suspension.

These observations, again, make no claim other than that of being conjectures that can be tested experimentally. However, I should not fail to direct your attention to the fact that it has become possible only through the concept of catalysts as accelerators that one can even postulate such conjectures that can be tested scientifically. I ask anyone to attempt something similar by means of molecular vibrations.

The Enzymes

Berzelius had no doubt that the conversion of starch into sugar by acids is to be put side by side with the conversion by malt extract. Payen and Persoz had the same idea; they isolated the effective substance, diastase, or at least produced it in concentrated form. The same holds for Liebig and Wöhler, who, in an outstanding experiment, studied the decomposition of amygdalin under the catalytic influence of emulsin.

The more recent investigations on the laws of enzyme action have, in my estimation, yielded nothing that would cause one to postulate any basic difference between the two types of action. On the contrary, Bredig's experiments, mentioned above, have made it possible to find much more thorough agreement than was to be expected.

We may thus regard the enzymes as catalysts that are created in the organism during the life of the cells and through whose action the living being disposes of the greatest portion of its tasks.

◆

16

LIMIT STATES AND
NORMAL CONDITIONS

New insight into heterogeneous catalysis was opened by the work
of Irving Langmuir (1881–1957). His experimental technique
was characterized by the use of very low pressures. Here is another instance where the study of "limit states" provided a good
starting point for understanding what happens under "normal"
conditions.

The interface between a solid substance and the surrounding
liquid or gas can be the site of a special action: less than a
chemical combination and more than a mere contact that leaves
the components unchanged. This special action is called "adsorption," and it forms the condition for catalysis.

What follows is a selection from the report presented by
Langmuir before the New York Section of the American Chemical Society in 1915.

◆

Chemical Reactions at Low Pressure [1]

IRVING LANGMUIR

In the course of investigations into the cause of the blackening of tungsten lamps, the effects produced by the introduction of low pressures of various gases have been studied in considerable detail.

It had been previously known that the vacuum in a lighted tungsten lamp normally improves during the life of the lamp, but it was thought that this removal of the residual gases was brought about by electrical discharges in much the same way as that commonly observed in Geissler and Roentgen-ray tubes. These experiments have shown, however, that a highly heated tungsten filament will cause the disappearance or cleanup of nearly any gas introduced into the bulb at low pressure and that this action, in the great majority of cases, is purely chemical in nature.

The experimental methods that have been employed in these investigations are relatively simple. A bulb containing one or more short filaments, usually of tungsten, was sealed to an apparatus consisting essentially of a mercury Gaede pump, a sensitive McLeod gauge for reading the pressures, and an apparatus for introducing small quantities of various gases into the system and for analyzing the gas residues obtained in the course of the experiments.

By means of the pump, the pressure in the system could be lowered to 0.00002 mm. of mercury. The McLeod gauge gave a reading of one millimeter on the scale for a pressure of 0.000007 mm. of mercury. By means of the apparatus for analyzing gas, a quantitative analysis of a single cubic millimeter (at atmospheric pressure) of gas could be carried out, determining the following

[1] *Journal of the American Chemical Society*, Vol. 37 (1915), pp. 1139–1167.

constituents: hydrogen, oxygen, carbon dioxide, carbon monoxide, nitrogen, and the inert gases.

The apparatus by which this has been accomplished had been in almost daily use for over five years, and during that time a very large number of reactions have been studied by its aid. In a typical experiment, after having thoroughly exhausted the whole apparatus, a small quantity, usually 5–20 mm. of gas, is introduced and the filament is electrically heated to a definite temperature, while readings of the pressure are taken at regular intervals (usually one minute). By plotting the pressure readings against the time, a curve is obtained which clearly shows how the rate of cleanup varies with the pressure.

A series of such curves are prepared with different filament temperatures and with various other changes in the conditions, which I shall describe later.

In this way we have studied the cleanup phenomena with many different gases and several different kinds of filaments. Most of the work has been done with tungsten filaments, but, in order to get a broader outlook over the field of low-pressure reactions, filaments of carbon, molybdenum, platinum, iron, palladium, and other metals have also been tried. The principal gases studied have been oxygen, nitrogen, hydrogen, carbon monoxide and dioxide, chlorine, bromine, iodine, methane, cyanogen, hydrochloric acid, argon, phosphine, and the vapors of many substances, such as mercury, phosphorus pentoxide, sulphur, etc.

With each of these gases, conditions can be found under which a heated tungsten filament will cause the cleanup of the gas. The curves obtained in the course of the experiments have furnished very complete data for a study of the kinetics of the reactions involved.

It has long been generally recognized that the kinetics of gas reactions afford the best, if not the only, means of studying the mechanism of reactions, and the literature of recent years shows that the velocities of many reactions have been investigated with this end in view.

Very few experimenters, however, have realized that by working with gases at extremely low pressures the experimental conditions may be enormously simplified, and the velocity of the reaction is then much more intimately related to the behavior of the individual molecule than it is at higher pressures.

In fact, by working continually with gases at these low pressures, one soon acquires an entirely new viewpoint and sees almost daily fresh evidences of the atomic and molecular structure of matter. The kinetic theory of gases then becomes the great guiding principle. According to this viewpoint, the velocity of a reaction is a matter of statistics. The question becomes: Out of all the gas molecules which strike the surface of a heated filament, what fraction enters into reaction with it?

This statistical viewpoint has become prevalent among physicists within the last few years. Without it, the tremendous advances in our knowledge of radioactivity, electric conduction through gases, applications of the quantum theory, etc., would have been impossible.

In the field of chemistry, however, only a very small beginning has been made. Chemistry was the first of the sciences to make use of the atomic theory, and, in fact, the history of chemistry in the last century shows that the great advances in both inorganic and organic chemistry were largely dependent on this theory.

The development of physical chemistry, however, took place along rather different lines. The remarkable progress which occurred from 1870 to 1900 was, in a large degree, based upon the applications of thermodynamics to chemistry. Gradually the idea became prevalent that the atomic theory was only a working hypothesis and might perhaps profitably be dispensed with entirely. The energy relations of reactions, on the other hand, were considered to be of the most fundamental importance. Just about the time that the majority of physical chemists had been won over to this viewpoint, the physicists began to discover absolute proofs of the existence of atoms and molecules and soon showed what remarkable results could be obtained by the applications of statistical methods.

As yet, apparently, very few chemists have awakened to the wonderful opportunities that lie open to them on all sides when they attack the problems of chemistry by the new methods which the physicists have developed. The physicist, on the other hand, is gradually beginning to extend his investigations into the field of the chemist, and we may hope, if the chemist will but meet him halfway, that there will result a new physical chemistry which will have an even more far-reaching effect on our ordinary chemical conceptions than has the physical chemistry of the last decades.

Perhaps the most noteworthy of the recent attempts to apply statistical methods to chemical changes is the work of J. J. Thomson on positive rays.

An excellent example of the study of chemical reactions by statistical methods, and this time by a chemist, is to be found in the work of S. C. Lind * on the nature of chemical action brought about by radioactive bodies.

The reactions we are to consider . . . are for the most part reactions between gases and heated filaments; that is, they are heterogeneous reactions involving a solid and gaseous phase. The kinetics of reactions of this type have not received the attention that has been accorded to homogeneous reactions. For example, in Jellinek's recent book *Physical Chemistry of Gas Reactions* [Leipzig: 1913], 34 pages are devoted to the kinetics of homogeneous reactions, but only half of one page to the kinetics of heterogeneous reactions.

It was at first thought that the law of mass action could be applied to heterogeneous reactions just as to homogeneous reactions. Experiments soon showed, however, that other factors than purely chemical ones usually determined the velocity of these reactions. Noyes and Whitney studied the rate of solution of solid substances in liquids and concluded that the velocity was de-

* *Journal of Physical Chemistry*, Vol. 16 (1912), p. 564.

pendent entirely on the rate at which the dissolved substances could diffuse through the thin layer of liquid next to the solid. Stirring the liquid had the effect of thinning this layer and so increased the rate.

Nernst extended this idea and suggested that the velocity of heterogeneous reactions in general was limited by the rate of diffusion of the reacting substances through a "diffusion layer," which he considered, under ordinary circumstances, to be of constant thickness. Thus he reasoned that the velocity of these reactions, in practically all cases, should be proportional to the concentration of the reacting substances. In other words, the reactions should follow the laws of monomolecular reactions. Nernst pointed out, however, that it was wrong to draw conclusions as to the mechanism of heterogeneous reactions from measurements of their velocity.

Fink, as a result of his study of the kinetics of the sulphur trioxide contact process, developed a theory of the mechanism that marked a new step in our conceptions of the mechanism of heterogeneous reactions. Bodenstein and Fink successfully applied this theory to a large number of other catalytic reactions.

This theory differs essentially from Nernst's, in that the reaction velocity is assumed to be limited by the rate of diffusion of the reacting bodies through an *adsorbed film* of *variable thickness*. Thus, in the case of the reaction

$$2SO_2 + O_2 = 2SO_3$$

in contact with platinum it is shown that there is present on the platinum an absorbed layer of SO_3. The theory assumes that the thickness of this layer is at all times proportional to the square root of the concentration of SO_3 in the gas phase; in other words, that there is an adsorption equilibrium. The reaction is assumed to take place only at the boundary between the adsorption film and the platinum. The oxygen and sulphur dioxide must therefore diffuse through the film before being able to react. In this way the theory indicates that the velocity of the reaction should be inversely proportional to the square root of the concentration of SO_3 and should be proportional either to the concentration of oxygen or to that of the sulphur dioxide (not to both), depending upon which is in excess at the surface of the platinum.

This theory seems to have met with general favor and has been applied to the kinetics of many heterogeneous reactions.

The experiments on gas reactions at low pressures which I shall describe . . . have shown that this theory must be modified and that we must consider the reaction velocity to be limited not by the rate of diffusion through the adsorbed film but rather by the rate at which the surface of the metal becomes exposed by the evaporation of single molecules from an adsorbed layer one molecule deep. We shall see that the statistical viewpoint will lead us very much further in the understanding of all reactions of this type.

We shall refer frequently to low gas pressures, and it will be well at the outset to say a word as to the unit of pressure which we shall use throughout. It has been customary to measure pressures in millimeters of mercury, but this is really a very arbitrary and inconvenient unit for such work as this. Professor Richards, last year at Cincinnati, made a strong appeal to chemists to use the C. G. S. unit of pressure, the *bar*, or the megabar, and enumerated many good reasons for doing so. The *bar* is defined as a pressure of one dyne per sq. cm., and the megabar is a million times this. The megabar is almost exactly 750 mm. of mercury and is really more nearly average atmospheric pressure than the 760 mm. usually adopted as standard. A bar is therefore one millionth of an atmosphere, or just three-fourths of a thousandth of a millimeter of mercury. This unit is particularly convenient for our purpose, for the pressures we shall deal with are usually from 1 to 100 bars.

We are now in a position to consider more in detail the reactions which occur when a gas is "cleaned up" by a heated filament. These reactions may be divided into four distinct classes, which we shall consider separately. The four types of reaction are those in which:

1. The filament is attacked by the gas.

2. The gas reacts with the vapor given off by the filament.

3. The filament acts catalytically on the gas, producing a chemical change in the gas without any permanent change in the filament.

4. The gas is chemically changed or is made to react with the filament by means of electrical discharges through the gas.

Cleanup of Oxygen by a Tungsten Filament

The action of oxygen on a tungsten filament is one of the best examples of this type of reaction. In air at atmospheric pressure, tungsten begins to oxidize at about 400–500° C. and becomes coated with an iridescent film, much as steel does. At higher temperatures, the oxidation becomes rapid and a scale of the yellow oxide WO_3 forms on the metal. At temperatures above 1500° K., the oxide volatilizes so rapidly that it forms a dense, white smoke. Under such conditions, the rate of oxidation evidently depends on the rate at which the oxygen can diffuse up to the surface of the metal through the nitrogen and through the layer of oxide on the surface. Such a large number of factors is involved that it would seem very difficult to derive much information as to the mechanism of the chemical reaction from experiments at these high pressures.

The case is quite different, however, when we study the action of a heated tungsten filament on oxygen at a pressure as low as, say, 100 bars. We then find that at temperatures above about 1200° K. the tungsten is attacked, producing the yellow oxide WO_3, but that this distills off as fast as it is formed, leaving the surface clean and bright.

Reactions between Chlorine and Tungsten

Chlorine at low pressures attacks tungsten, forming WCl_6. The velocity of the reaction reaches a maximum at about 1500° K.

and becomes extremely small at higher temperatures. This is undoubtedly to be explained by the dissociation of some of the intermediate products which are necessary steps in the formation of WCl_6. The chlorine leaving the filament is largely dissociated into atoms under these conditions and produces some extremely interesting effects which I shall discuss more in detail a little later.

Reactions between Carbon and Oxygen

It has long been a disputed question whether carbon monoxide is a direct product of the oxidation of carbon or whether it is formed only by the interaction of carbon with carbon dioxide produced as a primary product.

By heating a carbon filament in oxygen at very low pressures in a bulb immersed in liquid air, a definite answer to this question is readily obtained. If carbon dioxide is produced and leaves the filament, it must travel directly to the bulb and there be condensed at the low temperature of liquid air where the vapor pressure of carbon dioxide is barely measurable. The filament therefore never comes in contact with carbon dioxide.

The first experiments showed that the phenomena involved in the oxidation of carbon are very complex as compared with those of the oxidation of tungsten. With tungsten, the results were always accurately reproducible, but with the carbon filaments the rate of cleanup depended entirely upon the previous history of the filament.

In the experiments, metalized carbon filaments were used. These consist of a highly graphitized carbon of the highest attainable purity (ash about 0.01 per cent). After mounting in the lamp, the filament was heated in a high vacuum for several hours until it ceased giving off measurable quantities of gas. Small quantities of oxygen at a pressure about 5–10 bars were admitted and the rate of cleanup with different filament temperatures was noted.

With the filament at 1220° K., the oxygen began to disappear very rapidly, but soon slowed down to a rather uniform slow rate. At this temperature, the whole of the oxygen gradually disappeared and CO_2, without a trace of CO, was formed. The amount of CO_2, however, was considerably less than the equivalent of the oxygen that disappeared. On adding a second supply of oxygen, the rate of cleanup was very much slower than the first time. After three or four treatments, the rate of cleanup finally became reproducible. On raising the filament temperature to 1700° K., the rate of cleanup increased again, but gradually decreased as before.

Clean-up of Oxygen by Platinum

A platinum filament at temperatures above about 1600° K. gradually causes the cleanup of low pressures of oxygen. With pressures less than 100 or 200 bars, the rate is independent of the pressure. The filament loses weight at the same rate as in vacuum. Quantitative measurements show that the oxygen combines with the platinum atoms as fast as they evaporate from the filament and form the compound PtO_2, which collects on the bulb as a brown deposit. At higher pressures, the oxygen also begins to attack the platinum at a rate dependent on the pressure.

Dissociation of Hydrogen into Atoms

It has been shown that when a wire of tungsten, platinum, or palladium is heated to a temperature above 1300° K. in hydrogen at very low pressure (1–20 bars), a portion of the hydrogen molecules that strike the filament is dissociated into atoms. This atomic hydrogen has remarkable properties. It is readily adsorbed by glass surfaces at room temperature, although more strongly at liquid-air temperatures; but only a very small amount (a few cu. mm.) can be so retained because the atoms evidently react together to form molecular hydrogen as soon as they come in contact, even at liquid-air temperatures. The atomic hydrogen reacts instantly at room temperature with oxygen, phosphorus, and many reducible substances, such as WO_3, PtO_2, etc.

When a tungsten wire is heated to very high temperatures (above 2000°) in hydrogen, the dissociation of the gas in contact with the wire causes the absorption of a very large quantity of heat. The atomic hydrogen produced diffuses out from the wire and as soon as it reaches a cooler region recombines to form molecules and liberates the heat of the reaction. The result is that the heat conductivity of hydrogen, at temperatures where dissociation occurs, is several times larger than it would otherwise be.

Dissociation of Chlorine into Atoms

By heating a tungsten filament for a short time to 3000° K. in a high vacuum, a sufficient quantity volatizes to form a black deposit on the bulb. If, now, a low pressure of chlorine be admitted to the bulb, this does not perceptibly attack the deposit on the bulb or the filament, even if the bulb is heated to 200° C. However, if the filament is now heated to a high temperature while the bulb is kept cool, the tungsten deposit on the bulb soon disappears. The chlorine has evidently been activated or dissociated by the filament, and the atoms formed travel at these low pressures directly from the filament to the bulb without having any chance to recombine on the way.

The experiment is more striking if two filaments be placed side by side in the same bulb containing a very low pressure of chlorine. If one of the filaments be heated to a high temperature, it is found that the other one, which remains cold, is gradually eaten away on the side facing the hot filament until it finally disappears completely. The hot one does not lose at all in weight, but may even become heavier, by having tungsten deposited on it by the decomposition of the chloride formed by the attack of the cold filament.

Dissociation of Oxygen into Atoms

In connection with the cleanup of oxygen by a tungsten filament, I have already spoken of some of the evidence for the dissociation of oxygen into atoms at extremely low pressures. Still better evidence has been obtained in some experiments on thermionic currents in which the bulb containing the filaments is immersed in liquid air. Under these conditions, an active form of oxygen can be collected on the glass which is slowly given off and reacts even at liquid-air temperatures with tungsten. The phenomena are in many ways similar to those observed with hydrogen. A further quantitative study of the formation of this active oxygen is being undertaken.

Reaction between Carbon Monoxide and Oxygen in Contact with Platinum

In all the reactions I have spoken of thus far, there has been only one gas in contact with the filament. The case where the filament acts catalytically on a reaction between two gases is an important one and warranted special study. For this purpose, a short filament of fine platinum wire was mounted in the center of a four-liter bulb. Pressures of carbon monoxide and oxygen up to a total of about 30 bars were admitted, and the filament was heated to such a temperature that the reaction proceeded at a convenient rate. A large tube extended from the lower part of the bulb and was kept immersed in liquid air, so that the molecules of carbon dioxide produced in the reaction were condensed before they had any opportunity of striking the filament.

The results were very striking. The rate of cleanup was found to be directly proportional to the pressure of oxygen, but *inversely proportional* to the pressure of carbon monoxide.

Reaction between Hydrogen and Oxygen
in Contact with Platinum

This reaction proves at low pressures in absence of water vapor to be essentially similar to that between carbon monoxide and oxygen. At low temperatures, the rate of reaction is directly proportional to the pressure of oxygen and *inversely proportional to that of the hydrogen.* At higher temperatures, the rate varies with the pressure, . . . but in contrast to the behavior of oxygen and carbon monoxide, the velocity does not decrease when the temperature is raised even to the melting point of the filament.

◆

17

OUTLOOK
AND CONCLUSION

It has a special meaning that this book ends with the topic of catalysis. The research efforts reported and reviewed in this book have acted as catalysts in the ensuing great developments in chemical science and technology: the elucidation of the arrangements in which atoms combine to form complex molecules; the insight into the structure of natural substances; the synthesis of dyestuffs and drugs; the production of plastics by condensation and polymerization; the recognition of agents and reactions in the life processes of organisms; the interconversions between chemical and electrical energy; the discovery of atomic energy and its tremendous consequences in war and peace.

These developments require from us a factual awareness of where we are, and knowing the paths by which we got there will help us to determine where they should lead.

BIBLIOGRAPHY

HISTORY AND BIOGRAPHY

FARBER, EDUARD, *The Evolution of Chemistry* (New York: Ronald, 1952).
——— (ed.), *Great Chemists* (New York: Interscience—Wiley, 1961).
———, *Nobel-Prize Winners in Chemistry*, rev. ed. (New York: Abelard-Schuman, 1962).
IHDE, AARON J., *The Development of Modern Chemistry* (New York, Evanston, London: Harper & Row, 1964).
LEICESTER, HENRY M., and KLICKSTEIN, HERBERT S., *A Source Book in Chemistry 1400–1900* (New York: McGraw-Hill, 1952).
PARTINGTON, J. R., *A Short History of Chemistry*, 3d ed. (New York: Harper Torchbooks, 1960).
———, *A History of Chemistry*, 4 vols. (London: Macmillan; New York: St. Martin's Press, 1961–1966).

GENERAL AND INORGANIC CHEMISTRY

ANDREWS, D. H., and KOKES, R. J., *Fundamental Chemistry* (New York: Wiley, 1962).
BRESCIA, F., ARENTS, J., MEISLICH, H., and TURK, A., *Fundamentals of Chemistry: a Modern Introduction* (New York: Academic Press, 1966).
HILDEBRAND, J., and POWELL, R. E., *Principles of Chemistry*, 7th ed. (New York: Macmillan, 1964).
NATHANS, MARCEL W., *Elementary Chemistry* (Englewood Cliffs, N.J.: Prentice-Hall, 1963).
PAULING, LINUS, *General Chemistry*, 2d ed. (San Francisco: W. H. Freeman and Co., 1953).
———, *The Architecture of Molecules* (San Francisco: W. H. Freeman & Co., 1964).
ROSE, ARTHUR, and ROSE, ELIZABETH, *Condensed Chemical Dictionary*, 6th ed. (New York; Reinhold, 1961).
SISLER, H. H., VANDERWERF, C. A., and DAVIDSON, A. W., *General Chemistry, a Systematic Approach*, 2d ed. (New York: Macmillan, 1959).

ABOUT ATOMS AND ELEMENTS

ASIMOV, ISAAC, *The Search for the Elements* (New York: Basic Books, 1962).

FRISCH, OTTO R., *Atomic Physics Today* (New York: Basic Books, 1961).

HUTCHINSON, ERIC, *Chemistry: The Elements and Their Reactions* (Philadelphia: Saunders, 1959).

SISLER, HARRY H., *Electronic Structure, Properties, and the Periodic Law* (New York: Reinhold, 1963).

WEEKS, MARI ELVIRA, and LEICESTER, HENRY M., *Discovery of the Elements*, 6th ed. (Easton, Pa.: Chemical Education Publishing Co., 1956).

WHYTE, LANCELOT LAW, *Essay on Atomism: From Democritus to 1960* (Middletown, Conn.: Wesleyan University Press, 1961).

PHYSICAL CHEMISTRY

BENSON, S. W., *Foundations of Chemical Kinetics* (New York: McGraw-Hill, 1960).

DANIELS, F., and ALBERTY, R. A., *Physical Chemistry*, 2d ed. (New York: Wiley, 1961).

GLASSTONE, S., *Textbook of Physical Chemistry* (Princeton, N.J.: Van Nostrand, 1946).

LAIDLER, K. J., *Chemical Kinetics* (New York: McGraw-Hill, 1950).

LEWIS, G. N., and RANDALL, M., rev. by K. S. PITZER and L. BREWER, *Thermodynamics* (New York: McGraw-Hill, 1961).

MAHAN, BRUCE H., *Elementary Chemical Thermodynamics* (New York: W. A. Benjamin, 1963).

MARON, SAMUEL H., and PRUTTON, CARL F., *Principles of Physical Chemistry* (New York: Macmillan, 1965).

MOELWYN-HUGHES, E. A., *Physical Chemistry*, 2d ed., rev. (New York: Macmillan, 1960).

NASH, LEONARD, *Elements of Chemical Thermodynamics* (Reading, Mass.: Addison-Wesley, 1962).

SEMENOV, N. N., *Some Problems of Chemical Kinetics and Reactivity* (New York: Macmillan, 1959).

INDEX